DO Drops

Volume 2

DO Drops
Volume 2

Daily Bible Devotional

Dr. Bo Wagner

Word of His Mouth Publishers
Mooresboro, NC

All Scripture quotations are taken from the **King James Version** of the Bible.

ISBN: 978-1-941039-20-5
Printed in the United States of America
©2019 Dr. Bo Wagner (Robert Arthur Wagner)

Word of His Mouth Publishers
Mooresboro, NC 28114
www.wordofhismouth.com

Cover art by Chip Nuhrah

Devotion 1

The book of Judges, with all of its sordid wickedness, is behind us. We now arrive in the glorious book of Ruth. And while the events of the book of Ruth took place during the time period of the Judges, the tone of the book could not be more different. At the outset, though, we are once again faced with an episode of disobedience brought on by a lack of faith.

The book opens with the family of a man named Elimelech that lived in Bethlehem. A famine arose, and Elimelech made a horrible decision; he and his family would ride things out in the foreign land of Moab. The people and land of Moab were not for the people of God; the Moabites had a bad background, bad beliefs, and bad behavior. Elimelech, though, rationalized all of this away by the use of a word found in verse one:

Ruth 1:1 *Now it came to pass in the days when the judges ruled, that there was a famine in the land. And a certain man of Beth-lehem-judah went to sojourn in the country of Moab, he, and his wife, and his two sons.*

Sojourn. It means "to visit for a while." But by the time we get to verse two, we find that "sojourned" had become "continued," and by the time we get to verse four, "continued" had become "dwelled." A matter of backsliding that Elimelech determined to be temporary became very much permanent. It usually does.

DO recognize that backsliding by its very nature tends toward permanence. That being the case, the wisest thing we can ever do is never backslide to begin with even in ways that seem "small" or even "sensible!"

Personal Notes:

_____

_____

_____

_____

_____

_____

_____

_____

_____

_____

_____

_____

_____

_____

_____

_____

_____

_____

_____

_____

_____

_____

_____

_____

_____

_____

_____

_____

Devotion 2

After the family of Elimelech had been in Moab for a while, tragedy struck; Elimelech died. Then after many more years, tragedy struck yet again:

Ruth 1:5 *And Mahlon and Chilion died also both of them; and the woman was left of her two sons and her husband.*

When Naomi came into Moab, it was with a husband and two sons. The arrangement was specifically supposed to be temporary; they would all be there just a little while, then they would all go home. But those intentions were no comfort to Naomi as she wept bitter tears over three graves in the land of Moab. The three men of the family never made it home. Yes, this is tragic. But it is also literally the most predictable thing in the entire human experience; everyone dies! There was never a question of whether Elimelech, Mahlon, and Chilion were going to die; the only question is where would they be when it happened. If they wanted to be assured of never DYING in Moab, the logical course was never to begin LIVING in Moab.

Unless the rapture comes, every one of us is going to die. The question therefore becomes, will we die in God's will or out of God's will? Will we stand before Him thrilled, or will we stand before Him embarrassed? Will we be rewarded, or will we be empty-handed?

DO live in God's will every day; it is a flawless way to make sure that you also die in His will!

Personal Notes:

_____

_____

_____

_____

_____

_____

_____

_____

_____

_____

_____

_____

_____

_____

_____

_____

_____

_____

_____

_____

_____

_____

_____

_____

_____

_____

_____

Devotion 3

Naomi heard that God had visited Bethlehem. Bread was filling the land once again; the famine was over. And so, having already lost her husband and both sons to death in Moab, she determined to make her way back across the Jordan into her homeland once again. But before she did, she had some family ties to break. Before their death, both of her boys had gotten married to Moabite girls. Naomi had two daughters-in-law to say goodbye to. As she said goodbye, notice how she praised these girls:

Ruth 1:8 *And Naomi said unto her two daughters in law, Go, return each to her mother's house: the Lord deal kindly with you, as ye have dealt with the dead, and with me.*

Naomi made special note of how good these girls had been both with her and with her boys. Were these girls Moabites? Yes. But had they been wonderfully kind? Yes again. Naomi would not let their pagan background keep her from being honest about their good qualities.

There is a needed and often a very difficult lesson in that. As Christians, are we to tell the often very negative truth about sin, about sinners, about sinful organizations? Yes, certainly. But if we ever intend to win sinners, we must also learn to be honest enough and kind enough to speak well of people when they deserve it, sinner or no! No sinner was ever won to God by hatefulness, but multitudes have been won by kindness.

DO speak the unpopular truth about sin. But DO speak any deservedly kind words about sinners as well!

Personal Notes:

_____

_____

_____

_____

_____

_____

_____

_____

_____

_____

_____

_____

_____

_____

_____

_____

_____

_____

_____

_____

_____

_____

_____

_____

_____

Devotion 4

Naomi was heading home. But before she left, she told her two daughters-in-law to stay there in Moab. She explained to them that based on the Jewish law of the kinsman redeemer, if she had any more sons or near relatives, they could expect someone to marry them if they came with her. But since she was now (she thought) totally bereft of family, they should not come; no one else would have anything to do with them since they were Moabites.

Both of the girls had vowed to go with her. But once she explained things, a divergent picture began to emerge:

Ruth 1:14 *And they lifted up their voice, and wept again: and Orpah kissed her mother in law; but Ruth clave unto her.*

Kissed. Clave. Orpah demonstrated emotion; Ruth demonstrated devotion. Emotion is always the easier of those two things. Emotion says, "I feel." Devotion says, "I am committed no matter how I feel." Emotion rises and falls on the circumstances of the day; devotion stays steady no matter the circumstances.

This, in a microcosm, is why some people can be counted on to be faithful, and others must constantly be prodded and petted and coddled. Some are emotional about God; some are devoted to God.

DO examine your walk with God; is it emotion-based or devotion based? Are you merely kissing Him, or are you truly cleaving to Him? Emotion will carry you only to the border of Moab. Devotion will carry you all the way across the Jordan and headlong into whatever uncertainties may lay ahead and from there into all of the blessings God has waiting for you at the end of the trial.

Personal Notes:

_____

_____

_____

_____

_____

_____

_____

_____

_____

_____

_____

_____

_____

_____

_____

_____

_____

_____

_____

_____

_____

_____

_____

_____

_____

_____

_____

_____

_____

Devotion 5

Orpah has kissed Naomi, turned around, and walked away. She will now disappear from the life of Naomi and from the pages of Scripture. But Ruth has not merely kissed Naomi, she has clung onto her and promised not to leave. So, Naomi tried again. She pointed out that Orpah had left and again encouraged Ruth to do the same. Ruth's response has become legendary, so much so that it is often repeated in weddings all of these thousands of years later. Verse sixteen gives us one half of it:

Ruth 1:16 *And Ruth said, Intreat me not to leave thee, or to return from following after thee: for whither thou goest, I will go; and where thou lodgest, I will lodge: thy people shall be my people, and thy God my God:*

The last phrase is the really key part: "and thy God my God." Ruth was willingly and openly forsaking the false gods of Moab and wholly placing her trust in the God of Israel. In so doing, she became an amazing picture of the requirements of New Testament salvation.

Simply put, it is not just faith in Christ; it is faith in Christ ALONE! It can only be Him, not Him along with some other him, not Him added to our good works, just Him, only Him. DO examine what you mean when you say, "I am saved." If there is anything added to Him, then you have a very fatally flawed view of salvation!

Personal Notes:

_____
_____
_____
_____
_____
_____
_____
_____
_____
_____
_____
_____
_____
_____
_____
_____
_____
_____
_____
_____
_____
_____
_____
_____
_____
_____
_____
_____
_____

Devotion 6

When Naomi walked back into Bethlehem, the entire city was moved about her. They spoke to her, calling her by name. Her name, by the way, meant "sweetness." Instantly Naomi bristled at that. She demanded to be called Marah instead, which means "bitter." She then explained her demand:

Ruth 1:21 *I went out full, and the Lord hath brought me home again empty: why then call ye me Naomi, seeing the Lord hath testified against me, and the Almighty hath afflicted me?*

The bitterness of Naomi is the unmissable 900-pound gorilla in the room. But please look past that for a moment, because there is actually something much more important to see. Naomi said, "I went out full." Many years earlier, the family had left fearing the famine and seeing nothing in Bethlehem worth staying for. But now, coming home empty-handed, she looks backs and says, "I had everything!" So, if they had everything, why did they leave to begin with?

Does it not often seem that people do not realize what they have until it is gone? They stray from the will of God seeking some elusive thing they think they simply must have, and it is not until they lose everything that they realize that they actually had everything.

In the retail world, there is something called an inventory. A company will stop business for a day or two simply to count and see what they already have. I think sometimes it would be good for Christians to emulate that habit. If people did an inventory of the blessings of God in their lives, they would likely be much less likely to stray away looking for something else.

DO take time, either on paper or in your head or just on your knees to do an inventory. Take stock of every precious thing and person God has placed in your life. People who are busy counting their blessings are not usually people straying away from God's will looking for better things in the devil's lands.

Personal Notes:

_____

_____

_____

_____

_____

_____

_____

_____

_____

_____

_____

_____

_____

_____

_____

_____

_____

_____

_____

_____

_____

Devotion 7

Once Naomi and Ruth had gotten back to Bethlehem, a problem presented itself. They were two widows, one young and one old, with great debts and no provider. But Ruth, knowing the law of Moses and the customs of the land, understood that she was allowed to go out into the field of perfect strangers and glean after the reapers. In so doing, hard-working people could put food on the table for their family.

Mind you, though, Ruth knew absolutely no one in the area. Notice what Ruth 2:3 says happened to her that day:

Ruth 2:3 *And she went, and came, and gleaned in the field after the reapers: and her hap was to light on a part of the field belonging unto Boaz, who was of the kindred of Elimelech.*

The word "hap" is the word from which we get our modern word happenstance. In other words, it "just so happened" that she ended up in the field of a man by the name of Boaz. It was, by all appearances, just a "coincidence."

But we know quite clearly from the rest of the book that what she viewed as coincidence was absolutely the providential will of God. Without even knowing where she was going, she landed in the field of the man who would be her husband and kinsman redeemer.

DO realize that people who are in God's will have the most amazing "coincidences!" There is no life so adventurous and so well provided for as the life of a person living in God's will every single day.

Personal Notes:

_____
_____
_____
_____
_____
_____
_____
_____
_____
_____
_____
_____
_____
_____
_____
_____
_____
_____
_____
_____
_____
_____
_____
_____
_____
_____
_____
_____

Devotion 8

Ruth had been working all day in the field. Toward the end of the day, the owner, Boaz, came out to the worksite to speak to the reapers. Look at the very first words we hear from the lips of Boaz in Scripture:

Ruth 2:4 *And, behold, Boaz came from Bethlehem, and said unto the reapers, The LORD be with you. And they answered him, The LORD bless thee.*

"The Lord be with you." To which they answered, "the Lord bless thee."

Mind you, this was not a religious service or even a religious setting. This was on the job during the workweek. And yet for Boaz, there was no division between the "secular" and the "sacred."

And there should not be. For a child of God, every day of our lives ought to be lived in light of the fact that we are children of God. The words that we speak ought to be godly; the attitudes that we portray ought to be godly; our behavior ought to be godly. When God needed a kinsman redeemer for precious Ruth, when He needed someone to be in the bloodline of His son, He did not choose a person who was coarse, ill-mannered, and of poor behavior. He chose a man who showed up at work and said, "the Lord be with you."

DO realize that God's expectations for our Christianity extend far beyond the walls of the church. If what we call Christianity is simply a Sunday thing, then it is not Christianity at all!

Personal Notes:

_____
_____
_____
_____
_____
_____
_____
_____
_____
_____
_____
_____
_____
_____
_____
_____
_____
_____
_____
_____
_____
_____
_____
_____
_____
_____
_____

Devotion 9

After Boaz had greeted his workers, his eyes lit on Ruth, and he instantly had a question:

Ruth 2:5 *Then said Boaz unto his servant that was set over the reapers, Whose damsel is this?*

His foreman quickly had an answer:

Ruth 2:6 *And the servant that was set over the reapers answered and said, It is the Moabitish damsel that came back with Naomi out of the country of Moab: 7 And she said, I pray you, let me glean and gather after the reapers among the sheaves: so she came, and hath continued even from the morning until now, that she tarried a little in the house.*

What did this foreman see in Ruth? Someone who was polite, someone who was hard-working, and someone who knew how to stick with it all day long. The way he described her would make any employer want to hire her on the spot.

This is exactly the type of character that God expects of His children, and the workplace is one of the greatest places to demonstrate it.

DO remember that advancement in God's sight comes through this very type of behavior. But it normally also comes in man's sight as well! Boaz's first impression of Ruth was a good one. The old saying "you never get a second chance to make a first impression" has a measure of truth to it. Behave yourself every day as if every impression you make is a first impression!

Personal Notes:

_____
_____
_____
_____
_____
_____
_____
_____
_____
_____
_____
_____
_____
_____
_____
_____
_____
_____
_____
_____
_____
_____
_____
_____
_____
_____
_____

Devotion 10

After Boaz had gotten the report on Ruth from his foreman, he began to speak to her. In verses eight and nine, he extended her grace and kindness far beyond the law of Moses. He was treating her as if she were the most special person in the world.

Her response to him indicated that she recognized that:

Ruth 2:10 *Then she fell on her face, and bowed herself to the ground, and said unto him, Why have I found grace in thine eyes, that thou shouldest take knowledge of me, seeing I am a stranger?*

Ruth was asking why. Why was he being so very kind to her? After all, she was just, in her own words, a "stranger." She was a Moabitess, a nobody.

This man's kindness to her broke down barriers in her heart and paved the way for all that God had in store for both of them.

DO realize as you go about your day that you will come in contact with people who have barriers in place in their heart, barriers that can only be broken down by the hammer of infinite kindness. Show that kindness; others may see a nobody, but God sees a potential Ruth.

Personal Notes:

_____

_____

_____

_____

_____

_____

_____

_____

_____

_____

_____

_____

_____

_____

_____

_____

_____

_____

_____

_____

_____

_____

_____

_____

_____

_____

_____

Devotion 11

After Boaz extended kindness and grace to Ruth, she asked him why. In verse eleven, he answered, and his answer is a beautiful thing:

Ruth 2:11 *And Boaz answered and said unto her, It hath fully been shewed me, all that thou hast done unto thy mother in law since the death of thine husband: and how thou hast left thy father and thy mother, and the land of thy nativity, and art come unto a people which thou knewest not heretofore.*

It hath been fully shewed me. Boaz, before he ever laid eyes on Ruth, had already heard about her in great detail. Her behavior had preceded her. If you have ever wondered why and how God softened the heart of a Jewish man to a Moabitess woman, understand that the process started right here. Before he ever knew whether she was short or tall or pretty or ugly, Boaz knew that she had great character and a tender heart.

Pretty is common; character is priceless.

DO determine to live your life in such a way that everyone who ever hears of you already thinks the world of you before they ever meet you, because if they think the world of you, it will be an easy thing for them to think the world of your God.

Personal Notes:

_____

_____

_____

_____

_____

_____

_____

_____

_____

_____

_____

_____

_____

_____

_____

_____

_____

_____

_____

_____

_____

_____

_____

_____

_____

_____

Devotion 12

After telling Ruth that he had heard all about her, her character, her compassion toward her family, he had one more thing to say to her, and he said so in the most picturesque of language:

Ruth 2:12 *The LORD recompense thy work, and a full reward be given thee of the LORD God of Israel, under whose wings thou art come to trust.*

Boaz described Ruth as having placed herself under the wings of the God of Israel. Multiple times in Scripture, God describes Himself in those types of terms, as a protective bird willing to spread the wings over the chicks.

I think we can all agree on a few things. One, life is hard. Two, trouble tends to come in bunches.

When you have those days where you feel like everything is beating down on you, remember that the very God of heaven, the King of kings, has His wings spread for you to come underneath His protection.

DO remember that if He was willing to allow a Moabitess under those wings, He is willing to allow us under them as well!

Personal Notes:

_____
_____
_____
_____
_____
_____
_____
_____
_____
_____
_____
_____
_____
_____
_____
_____
_____
_____
_____
_____
_____
_____
_____
_____
_____
_____
_____

Devotion 13

Boaz had spoken kindly to Ruth, and she had gone back out into the field once again to work. It is very likely that the servants of Boaz had been very surprised by his kindness to her, kindness that far exceeded the demands of the law. If they were surprised, though, they were about to become far more so:

Ruth 2:15 *And when she was risen up to glean, Boaz commanded his young men, saying, Let her glean even among the sheaves, and reproach her not: 16 And let fall also some of the handfuls of purpose for her, and leave them, that she may glean them, and rebuke her not.*

Boaz commanded that she be allowed to glean among the sheaves. This was considered "easy pickings," and was therefore customarily off limits. But he then shocked them even further by commanding that they drop handfuls in front of her, making her job of basket filling almost as easy as if it was happening with no effort. Then he told them neither to reproach nor rebuke her.

In other words, for Boaz it was not enough that he alone be extremely kind to others; he would not be satisfied until everyone responsible to him was that kind to others as well.

DO teach and expect kindness of those that are under you, be they children, employees, students, or anything else. Never allow anyone over whom you have any authority or influence to be anything less than extremely kind. A hurting world needs it, and God will hold us responsible for it.

Personal Notes:

_____
_____
_____
_____
_____
_____
_____
_____
_____
_____
_____
_____
_____
_____
_____
_____
_____
_____
_____
_____
_____
_____
_____
_____

Devotion 14

Ruth had finished her gleaning for the day and was coming home with way more than a full basket. The kindness of Boaz toward her had been so lavish that, when she arrived home, it was sure to attract the attention of Naomi:

Ruth 2:19 *And her mother in law said unto her, Where hast thou gleaned to day? and where wroughtest thou? blessed be he that did take knowledge of thee. And she shewed her mother in law with whom she had wrought, and said, The man's name with whom I wrought to day is Boaz.*

Boaz, no doubt, had only one thing in mind: being kind to Ruth. But his kindness had an unintended consequence: someone else noticed. He did not have to advertise; it simply was obvious to Naomi.

When we show kindness to others, there is almost always a multiplier effect. We get a blessing for doing so, the person we are kind to gets a blessing by our kindness, and others get a blessing by seeing it.

DO be kind; many actions have only the effect of addition, but kindness most always has the effect of multiplication!

Personal Notes:

_____

_____

_____

_____

_____

_____

_____

_____

_____

_____

_____

_____

_____

_____

_____

_____

_____

_____

_____

_____

_____

_____

_____

_____

_____

_____

_____

_____

Devotion 15

After Ruth came home with her abundant supply from Boaz, Naomi marveled over how kind someone had been to her. But when she asked who had done it, and Ruth answered, "A man named Boaz," Naomi was stunned in the best kind of way. Here was her response to Ruth:

Ruth 2:20 *And Naomi said unto her daughter in law, Blessed be he of the LORD, who hath not left off his kindness to the living and to the dead. And Naomi said unto her, The man is near of kin unto us, one of our next kinsmen.*

Naomi blessed the Lord. Ruth must have been utterly bewildered by her seemingly over-the-top reaction until Naomi explained what was going on. She told Ruth that Boaz was a near kinsman, next of kin, a potential kinsman redeemer.

In other words, the very thing she was absolutely certain that God could not provide, God did provide.

DO be careful never to sell God short. People often wander from His will for their lives, thinking that He will not be able to meet their needs. But God had Ruth's need provided before she ever left Moab, and He is just as able to meet our needs before we even get out of bed!

Personal Notes:

_____

_____

_____

_____

_____

_____

_____

_____

_____

_____

_____

_____

_____

_____

_____

_____

_____

_____

_____

_____

_____

_____

_____

_____

_____

_____

_____

_____

Devotion 16

Ruth continued to work in the field of Boaz, and she did so for approximately two months. The initial need of Naomi and Ruth when they came to Bethlehem was daily provision. Ruth, through her daily hard work, was amply providing that. Naomi could have continued comfortably in this arrangement for the rest of her life. But the compassion of Ruth for others had rubbed off on her.

Ruth 3:1 *Then Naomi her mother in law said unto her, My daughter, shall I not seek rest for thee, that it may be well with thee?*

Naomi was about to tell Ruth that she needed to approach Boaz about marrying her and fulfilling the role of the kinsman redeemer to her. If she did, and if he accepted, Naomi may well have been without any further provision for the rest of her life. But she was now willing to sacrifice her needs and desires for the needs and desires of Ruth.

And we know how that worked out! Not only was Ruth well provided for once Boaz married her, but Naomi was as well. She had no guarantees but was willing to do right by Ruth anyway.

DO be willing to put others before yourself. It is always right, and quite often, you will find that when you sacrifice for others, the Lord rewards you with even greater blessings than you could have ever imagined. Naomi gave up a daughter-in-law and ended up gaining an entire family, including a grandson!

Personal Notes:

_____
_____
_____
_____
_____
_____
_____
_____
_____
_____
_____
_____
_____
_____
_____
_____
_____
_____
_____
_____
_____
_____
_____
_____
_____
_____
_____
_____

Devotion 17

Naomi told Ruth to go to the end of the harvest party and prepare to propose to Boaz. If that sounds odd, the details to that proposal will sound even odder:

Ruth 3:3 *Wash thyself therefore, and anoint thee, and put thy raiment upon thee, and get thee down to the floor: but make not thyself known unto the man, until he shall have done eating and drinking.* **4** *And it shall be, when he lieth down, that thou shalt mark the place where he shall lie, and thou shalt go in, and uncover his feet, and lay thee down; and he will tell thee what thou shalt do.*

It is the last part of that proposal that sounds so incredibly odd. Naomi told Ruth to lay down at the feet of Boaz! Can you just imagine the hysterical reactions of today's modern feminist to that suggestion?

"How DARE you suggest I lay down at the stinking feet of some man! A woman is as good as any man; tell him to lay down at MY feet!"

But Ruth had a different spirit about her:

Ruth 3:5 *And she said unto her, All that thou sayest unto me I will do.*

That tender and humble spirit of Ruth is what won Boaz's heart to begin with. He already thought the world of her before he ever laid eyes on her. It is simply hard not to think the world of a person that humble and self-effacing.

DO determine that the most attractive thing about you will be your attitude. There is no amount of pretty that can make up for snottiness, and there is no

amount of ugly that cannot be made pretty by a tender
spirit!

Personal Notes:

_____
_____
_____
_____
_____
_____
_____
_____
_____
_____
_____
_____
_____
_____
_____
_____
_____
_____
_____
_____
_____
_____
_____
_____
_____
_____

Devotion 18

Naomi had told Ruth to go down to the threshing floor, uncover the feet of Boaz, and lay down at his feet. Ruth had responded, "All that thou sayest unto me I will do."

Have you ever found that is it easy to say something, but often much harder to follow through with it? A thing like this would surely fall into that category. So, how did Ruth do?

Ruth 3:6 *And she went down unto the floor, and did according to all that her mother in law bade her.7 And when Boaz had eaten and drunk, and his heart was merry, he went to lie down at the end of the heap of corn: and she came softly, and uncovered his feet, and laid her down.*

Ruth said she would do it...then she did it. She followed through on her commitment. And that decision resulted in her gaining the desires of her heart and walking into the pages of historical fame.

DO be a finisher. Anyone can determine to start something; it takes character to follow through!

Personal Notes:

_____

_____

_____

_____

_____

_____

_____

_____

_____

_____

_____

_____

_____

_____

_____

_____

_____

_____

_____

_____

_____

_____

_____

_____

_____

Devotion 19

In Ruth 3:7, Ruth had laid down at the feet of sleeping Boaz. At midnight Boaz woke up, afraid, wondering who in the world was in the room with him. When he asked, he got his answer. Ruth spoke and said, "I am Ruth, thine handmaid: spread therefore thy skirt over thine handmaid; for thou art a near kinsman."

She was proposing to Boaz. She was also a Moabitess. It would be an absolutely unthinkable thing for a Jewish man to marry a Moabitess, and yet she was asking him to do so anyway.

And look at his response.

Ruth 3:11 *And now, my daughter, fear not; I will do to thee all that thou requirest: for all the city of my people doth know that thou art a virtuous woman.*

Boaz agreed to marry her, and he did so based on one criterion; everyone knew that Ruth was a virtuous woman.

It was not her background that mattered to Boaz; it was her belief in God and her behavior that proved that belief in God.

DO remember every day that while you cannot change your background, your background does not determine your destination in life or in eternity! Your belief in God and behavior that proves it is far more powerful than your background could ever be, no matter how bad that background may be.

Personal Notes:

_____
_____
_____
_____
_____
_____
_____
_____
_____
_____
_____
_____
_____
_____
_____
_____
_____
_____
_____
_____
_____
_____
_____
_____
_____
_____
_____

Devotion 20

Ruth had done the most nerve-racking thing imaginable; she had proposed to Boaz. And almost immediately, her heart must have soared as she heard him agree to her proposal.

Have you ever been on a roller coaster? If you have, you know that your heart will be soaring one minute…and be jumping up into your throat the next as you plummet down toward the ground. That is exactly what happened to Ruth. Look at what Boaz said right after he told her that he would marry her:

Ruth 3:12 *And now it is true that I am thy near kinsman: howbeit there is a kinsman nearer than I.*

One minute Ruth was rejoicing in her heart over how thrilling it was about to be to become Mrs. Boaz; a split second later she was in anguish of mind realizing that she might not be able to get married to him after all, and may, in fact, have to marry some other man of whom she knew absolutely nothing!

Life is just like that, isn't it? To describe it as "uncertain" would be an understatement. One minute we are up, the next minute we are down; one minute we have hope, the next minute we are on pins and needles. How in the world could Ruth survive that, and how can we?

Because in Boaz's words, she had "come to trust under the wings of the God of Israel." It was not her circumstances that determined her outlook; it was her God that determined her outlook.

In this world of such great uncertainty, DO intentionally come to trust under the wings of God every single day. Winds and waves may change, but the wings of God are ever the same!

Personal Notes:

_____

_____

_____

_____

_____

_____

_____

_____

_____

_____

_____

_____

_____

_____

_____

_____

_____

_____

_____

_____

_____

_____

_____

_____

_____

_____

_____

Devotion 21

After telling Ruth that there was a kinsman who had the first right to marry her, Boaz did his best to assure her that things were going to come out right:

Ruth 3:13 *Tarry this night, and it shall be in the morning, that if he will perform unto thee the part of a kinsman, well; let him do the kinsman's part: but if he will not do the part of a kinsman to thee, then will I do the part of a kinsman to thee, as the LORD liveth: lie down until the morning.*

It is the last part of verse thirteen that is so fascinating to me at this point. Boaz told Ruth to stay right there at his feet until the morning.

Why would he say that?

The events of the book of Ruth took place during the time period of the judges, the most dangerous time period in all of Israel's history. To be out in the streets in the wee hours of the morning was an incredibly dangerous thing. But there at his feet, she was absolutely incomparably safe. The next day there would be a wedding, but for the time being, she was safe at his feet.

Do you see the beautiful parallel to the Christian life? We are betrothed to Christ. We will soon be married, but right now, each and every day, we are simply staying faithfully at His feet!

DO stay at His feet in the Word and in prayer and in fellowship and in church. The marriage supper of the Lamb is coming, but for right now, we can rejoice just in being at His feet!

Personal Notes:

_____

_____

_____

_____

_____

_____

_____

_____

_____

_____

_____

_____

_____

_____

_____

_____

_____

_____

_____

_____

_____

_____

_____

_____

_____

_____

_____

Devotion 22

Ruth did as Boaz requested and stayed at his feet until morning. But then, still early, before anyone else awoke, he loaded her up with produce and sent her back home to Naomi. When she arrived, Naomi was legitimately shocked to see her and asked her what seems to be a rather confusing question:

Ruth 3:16 *And when she came to her mother in law, she said, Who art thou, my daughter? And she told her all that the man had done to her.*

"Who are you?" What kind of question was that? Naomi knew who Ruth was. What she was asking was, "Who are you, Ruth? I was not expecting to see you home. Are you the woman who has been rejected? Are you the woman who has been told to wait for a while and let me think about it? What is going on?"

Her identity was tied up in the answer of Boaz.

Likewise, our identity is tied up in the answer of Christ. Who are we? If we received Him as our Lord and Savior, here is the answer:

1 John 3:2 *Beloved, now are we the sons of God, and it doth not yet appear what we shall be: but we know that, when he shall appear, we shall be like him; for we shall see him as he is.*

We, the saved, are already sons and daughters of God!

As you go about your day and as you face trials and troubles, DO remember who you are! This world may not see you as much; like Naomi, they may question your identity, but God already sees you as His son or His daughter!

Personal Notes:

_____
_____
_____
_____
_____
_____
_____
_____
_____
_____
_____
_____
_____
_____
_____
_____
_____
_____
_____
_____
_____
_____
_____
_____
_____
_____
_____
_____

Devotion 23

Ruth had come home, and Naomi had asked her who she was. Ruth explained the situation to her, informing her that there was, in fact, a second relative, a nearer relative, who had the right to marry her if he chose to do so.

At this point, Naomi knew what was going on in the heart of Boaz and what would happen next:

Ruth 3:18 *Then said she, Sit still, my daughter, until thou know how the matter will fall: for the man will not be in rest, until he have finished the thing this day.*

Naomi knew that Boaz would not wait a year or a month or a week or even a couple of days to deal with this. She knew that he "would not be in rest until he finished the thing this day." In other words, she knew that his highest priority was Ruth.

Boaz was a wealthy and very busy entrepreneur. He had ten thousand responsibilities and a million things to think of each day. And yet Ruth was his absolute highest priority; she was the thing foremost in his mind.

What a glorious picture of Christ and His love for us!

DO meditate every day on the fact that the God who holds the very universe together and has ten trillion things to think of each moment of every day has you first and foremost on His mind! You are not an item on the list to Him; He died for you; you ARE the list to Him!

Personal Notes:

_____
_____
_____
_____
_____
_____
_____
_____
_____
_____
_____
_____
_____
_____
_____
_____
_____
_____
_____
_____
_____
_____
_____
_____

Devotion 24

As Ruth waited back home with Naomi, Boaz made his way to the city gate. The gates of the city in those days were where government business was conducted and contracts were made. Boaz was on a mission to meet his only living relative and deal with the matter of Ruth.

And finally, he saw him coming by. When he did, he spoke to him, sort of. Look at the verse, and you will understand what I mean:

Ruth 4:1 *Then went Boaz up to the gate, and sat him down there: and, behold, the kinsman of whom Boaz spake came by; unto whom he said, Ho, such a one! turn aside, sit down here. And he turned aside, and sat down.*

Ho, such a one? What kind of greeting is that?

It is the kind of a greeting you give to a person whose name is not going to be important to history, a person who is about to shirk his duty as a kinsman redeemer. As we will see in the following verses over the next couple of devotions, this man refused to do his duty as a kinsman redeemer. As such, his name does not matter.

Importance is not nearly so much an issue of success and riches as it is a matter of faithfully doing what we ought to do.

DO determine not to be a "Ho, such a one." Let your name be remembered because you always did what was right!

Personal Notes:

_____

_____

_____

_____

_____

_____

_____

_____

_____

_____

_____

_____

_____

_____

_____

_____

_____

_____

_____

_____

_____

_____

_____

_____

_____

_____

_____

Devotion 25

Boaz was at the city gate, and "Ho Such A One" came by. Boaz had him sit down, and then he gathered ten men of the elders of the city. Court was now in session.

At that point, Boaz began to explain why he was there and what he wanted. He told the relative that there was a piece of land for sale, offered by the widow of Elimelech. This relative was first in line to buy it since he was the nearest living relative to the family.

The man quickly agreed to do so. But then Boaz pulled the ace out of his sleeve:

Ruth 4:5 *Then said Boaz, What day thou buyest the field of the hand of Naomi, thou must buy it also of Ruth the Moabitess, the wife of the dead, to raise up the name of the dead upon his inheritance.*

When "Ho Such A One" found out that he would have to marry Ruth in order to buy the piece of land, his tune suddenly changed:

Ruth 4:6 *And the kinsman said, I cannot redeem it for myself, lest I mar mine own inheritance: redeem thou my right to thyself; for I cannot redeem it.*

When the man said that marrying Ruth would "mar" his inheritance, he used a word of extreme disgust; he was practically throwing up on the ground at the thought of marrying Ruth. But why was he so cold toward her when Boaz was so fond of her?

Orpah. There were two young widows needing kinsman redeemers, and there were two potential kinsman redeemers available. Ruth was for Boaz; "Ho Such A One" was for Orpah. If she had come, God could have softened this man's heart toward her, just like He softened Boaz's heart toward Ruth.

DO remember that there is always enough for you in God's will even if you cannot see it! Ruth came to Bethlehem and found her kinsman redeemer; Orpah stayed in Moab and missed hers.

Personal Notes:

_____
_____
_____
_____
_____
_____
_____
_____
_____
_____
_____
_____
_____
_____
_____
_____
_____
_____
_____
_____
_____
_____
_____

Devotion 26

When the unnamed relative of Boaz refused to marry Ruth, an unusual transaction then took place at the gate:

Ruth 4:7 *Now this was the manner in former time in Israel concerning redeeming and concerning changing, for to confirm all things; a man plucked off his shoe, and gave it to his neighbour: and this was a testimony in Israel.* **8** *Therefore the kinsman said unto Boaz, Buy it for thee. So he drew off his shoe.*

A man had left home that day fully dressed. He ended up limping home that day missing a shoe. But that shoe was merely a representation of the fact that he had missed out on something much greater. He shirked his responsibility as a kinsman redeemer, and in so doing, missed out on becoming famous and ending up in the line of Christ! Yes, God planned Ruth for Boaz; but that does not change the fact that this man did not do what he was supposed to do.

What is his name? No one knows. Being "known" in God's eyes requires fulfilling the responsibilities He gives us.

DO realize each and every day that seemingly small choices to shirk the responsibilities that God gives us have the potential to make us miss out on the greatest blessings that He desired to give us!

Personal Notes:

_____

_____

_____

_____

_____

_____

_____

_____

_____

_____

_____

_____

_____

_____

_____

_____

_____

_____

_____

_____

_____

_____

_____

_____

_____

_____

_____

Devotion 27

After the unknown relative refused to marry Ruth, and after he pulled off his shoe and handed it to Boaz, Boaz had some things to say very publicly and very loudly:

Ruth 4:9 *And Boaz said unto the elders, and unto all the people, Ye are witnesses this day, that I have bought all that was Elimelech's, and all that was Chilion's and Mahlon's, of the hand of Naomi.* **10** *Moreover Ruth the Moabitess, the wife of Mahlon, have I purchased to be my wife, to raise up the name of the dead upon his inheritance, that the name of the dead be not cut off from among his brethren, and from the gate of his place: ye are witnesses this day.*

Mr. "Ho Such A One" was disgusted and embarrassed at the thought of marrying Ruth. Boaz was thrilled beyond measure at the opportunity to marry Ruth, and twice uttered the phrase, "ye are witnesses." Not only was he willing to marry Ruth, but he was also willing to let everyone know that everything he was doing was about her.

This, men, is the sign of a very good husband. There would never be a day that Ruth questioned the feelings of Boaz for her; he was all hers with no reservations.

Husbands, wives, DO let your spouse and the entire world know how you feel about your spouse. If there is ever a question in anyone's minds, then you are not doing your job!

Personal Notes:

_____

_____

_____

_____

_____

_____

_____

_____

_____

_____

_____

_____

_____

_____

_____

_____

_____

_____

_____

_____

_____

_____

_____

_____

_____

_____

_____

_____

Devotion 28

As the witnesses began to answer Boaz after his public proclamation that he was taking Ruth as his wife, they mentioned the names of some rather well-known people in Israel:

Ruth 4:11 *And all the people that were in the gate, and the elders, said, We are witnesses. The LORD make the woman that is come into thine house like Rachel and like Leah, which two did build the house of Israel: and do thou worthily in Ephratah, and be famous in Bethlehem:*

All of this was said in a public setting. Everyone that heard these words knew the names Rachel and Leah; those two women were icons in Israel, heroines to all the people. But since Ruth was a Moabitess, there were doubtless going to be some of the hearers there that day who scoffed at hearing her name mentioned in the same sentence as theirs. And that is very likely why the elders said what they said next:

Ruth 4:12 *And let thy house be like the house of Pharez, whom Tamar bare unto Judah, of the seed which the LORD shall give thee of this young woman.*

Tamar was on the opposite end of the spectrum from Rachel and Leah. She was the woman who pretended to be a prostitute and slept with her own father-in-law, Judah. And yet God used her offspring anyway to build the house of Israel. In other words, the elders were pointing out that someone's background, even a background as a pagan Moabitess, did not have to determine their future.

DO refrain from anchoring people to their family background in your mind. Everyone has skeletons way back in the family closet somewhere; what is really important, though, is where they are now and what direction they are heading!

Personal Notes:

_____

_____

_____

_____

_____

_____

_____

_____

_____

_____

_____

_____

_____

_____

_____

_____

_____

_____

_____

_____

_____

_____

_____

_____

_____

_____

Devotion 29

Since chapter two of the book of Ruth, Naomi has been fading into the background, and Ruth and Boaz have been taking center stage. But now, as the book draws near to a close, she is going to be mentioned in a very significant way once again.

Ruth 4:13 *So Boaz took Ruth, and she was his wife: and when he went in unto her, the LORD gave her conception, and she bare a son.* **14** *And the women said unto Naomi, Blessed be the LORD, which hath not left thee this day without a kinsman, that his name may be famous in Israel.* **15** *And he shall be unto thee a restorer of thy life, and a nourisher of thine old age: for thy daughter in law, which loveth thee, which is better to thee than seven sons, hath born him.* **16** *And Naomi took the child, and laid it in her bosom, and became nurse unto it.*

Naomi had been shattered by so many tragedies and reversals that she figured that her life was worthless and over. But by the time the book of Ruth comes to an end, she has reason after reason not just to keep on living but to actually enjoy life. She has a precious daughter-in-law, a new son-in-law, and now a new grandchild. She had been convinced that things would never get better...

But they did.

DO determine that no matter how bad circumstances seem, you will never give up hope. Naomi had no idea that any of this was even possible, but God had it all planned for her the entire time!

Personal Notes:

_____

_____

_____

_____

_____

_____

_____

_____

_____

_____

_____

_____

_____

_____

_____

_____

_____

_____

_____

_____

_____

_____

_____

_____

_____

_____

_____

_____

Devotion 30

The book of Ruth started with the famine and quickly devolved into a disaster for the family of Naomi and Elimelech. But look at how the book ends:

Ruth 4:16 *And Naomi took the child, and laid it in her bosom, and became nurse unto it. 17 And the women her neighbours gave it a name, saying, There is a son born to Naomi; and they called his name Obed: he is the father of Jesse, the father of David. 18 Now these are the generations of Pharez: Pharez begat Hezron, 19 And Hezron begat Ram, and Ram begat Amminadab, 20 And Amminadab begat Nahshon, and Nahshon begat Salmon, 21 And Salmon begat Boaz, and Boaz begat Obed, 22 And Obed begat Jesse, and Jesse begat David.*

David, as I am sure you know, was the greatest king Israel ever had. But he was just four generations removed from the disaster at the beginning of the book of Ruth. But when you look at it from the other side, this becomes a beautiful truth; the family of Naomi was just four generations removed from the greatness of King David! A family that thought they would never survive ended up achieving heights no one could have ever dreamed.

On the days where everything seems bleak and hopeless, DO realize that the greatest heights of greatness are still available for those people and families that just keep on putting one foot in front of the other and not quitting!

Personal Notes:

_____
_____
_____
_____
_____
_____
_____
_____
_____
_____
_____
_____
_____
_____
_____
_____
_____
_____
_____
_____
_____
_____
_____
_____
_____
_____
_____
_____

Devotion 31

The book of Ruth is behind us, and we are now entering the book of 1 Samuel, where the monarchy of Israel will begin. The first few chapters mark the last days of the Judges.

As the scene opens, we find a man going to Shiloh to worship the Lord and bringing both of his wives with him. This will be yet another example in Scripture of the disaster of polygamy. One of the wives, Peninah, has borne him several children, both multiple sons and multiple daughters. The other, Hannah, is barren. Peninah, for her part, is not all humble, and is, in fact, verbally abusive to Hannah over the situation, and we will observe more about that in the next devotion.

But it is the response of Elkanah, the husband, to all of this, that is so noteworthy.

1 Samuel 1:5 *But unto Hannah he gave a worthy portion; for he loved Hannah: but the LORD had shut up her womb.*

The greatest desire of a man's heart in Bible days was to have a son. Hannah was unable to give him the desire of his heart, and yet we find that he loved her anyway and treated her like gold. That is a perfect pattern for every child of God to follow in marriage.

DO determine, even when a spouse is not able to give you what you need or desire, that you will love them and treat them well. "They lived happily ever after" is usually preceded in real life by "they loved each other anyway."

Personal Notes:

_____

_____

_____

_____

_____

_____

_____

_____

_____

_____

_____

_____

_____

_____

_____

_____

_____

_____

_____

_____

_____

_____

_____

_____

_____

_____

_____

Devotion 32

We began yesterday looking at the family of Elkanah, especially his two wives Peninah and Hannah. We found that Peninah was producing a great many children, but Hannah was barren. But it is the attitude of Peninah that we want to examine at this point, and it was not a pleasant attitude.

1 Samuel 1:6 *And her adversary also provoked her sore, for to make her fret, because the LORD had shut up her womb.*

Peninah could not be content with rejoicing in the blessings of God in her own life; it seems that she could not be happy unless she was also making Hannah miserable at the exact same time. This was not a kind woman trying to encourage another one; Peninah was a horrible human being who made every day of life miserable for Hannah.

And that is the one and only thing we know about her!

Perhaps she was an excellent seamstress, or a great cook, or an early Israeli martial arts expert; we simply do not know. All we know of her is that she was mean. The snotty attitude that she exhibited in the privacy of her own home has been on display for all of humanity to see in Scripture for thousands of years now.

DO realize that God is not in the habit of allowing "mean" to go unnoticed and even unpublicized. It would be better to be kind and unknown than mean and infamous.

Personal Notes:

_____

_____

_____

_____

_____

_____

_____

_____

_____

_____

_____

_____

_____

_____

_____

_____

_____

_____

_____

_____

_____

_____

_____

_____

_____

_____

_____

Devotion 33

After being informed of the meanness of Peninah, her name disappears entirely from Scripture. She is never mentioned again by name, and I say, "Good riddance."

But the hurt she inflicted on Hannah was deep. Fortunately (other than the fact that he was dumb enough to have more than one wife), Elkanah was a brilliant and amazing husband.

1 Samuel 1:7 *And as he did so year by year, when she went up to the house of the LORD, so she provoked her; therefore she wept, and did not eat.* **8** *Then said Elkanah her husband to her, Hannah, why weepest thou? and why eatest thou not? and why is thy heart grieved? am not I better to thee than ten sons?*

Because of what Peninah was doing, Hannah was so brokenhearted that she was weeping and not eating. But in verse eight, we find her husband actually noticing the fact that she was weeping and that she was not eating. But the verse goes just a bit farther and shows us that he also noticed that her heart was grieved, and he knew the exact reason why her heart was grieved.

In other words, this man paid close attention to his wife.

Husbands, wives, you may be too poor to pay the bills, but no one is too poor to pay attention. Paying attention is free, and it just may save a marriage.

DO pay attention!

Personal Notes:

_____
_____
_____
_____
_____
_____
_____
_____
_____
_____
_____
_____
_____
_____
_____
_____
_____
_____
_____
_____
_____
_____
_____
_____
_____
_____
_____

Devotion 34

As the family continued their period of worship in Shiloh, Hannah continued to experience anguish of soul. Fortunately, she was a wise enough woman to know exactly where to take her sorrows and hurts:

1 Samuel 1:10 *And she was in bitterness of soul, and prayed unto the LORD, and wept sore.* **11** *And she vowed a vow, and said, O LORD of hosts, if thou wilt indeed look on the affliction of thine handmaid, and remember me, and not forget thine handmaid, but wilt give unto thine handmaid a man child, then I will give him unto the LORD all the days of his life, and there shall no razor come upon his head.*

Like a great many people, Hannah went to the Lord in prayer and did so in "bargaining mode." She wanted something from the Lord and was willing to give something to the Lord. But the great difference between Hannah and people today in the bargains that they usually make with the Lord is that her bargain had nothing at all to do with salvation or service.

Most vows that people make before the Lord today are something along the lines of "if you heal from disease or rescue from trouble, then I will believe in You and/or obey You." But this was not the bargain Hannah made. She already believed in the Lord. She already served Him. Her bargain was simply, "If you bless me with what I ask, I will turn right around and give that blessing back to you."

That is the right kind of bargain when it is God with whom you are bargaining.

DO ask God for what you desire, but do not ever make salvation or service a bargaining chip. Salvation is the free gift of God purchased with His blood, and service to the God who saved us is the least we can do whether He ever gives us a single blessing beyond salvation or not!

Personal Notes:

_____

_____

_____

_____

_____

_____

_____

_____

_____

_____

_____

_____

_____

_____

_____

_____

_____

_____

_____

_____

_____

_____

_____

_____

Devotion 35

As Hannah continued to kneel before the throne of heaven and pour her heart out to God, it turned out that she was being watched, and not just by heaven:

1 Samuel 1:12 *And it came to pass, as she continued praying before the LORD, that Eli marked her mouth.* **13** *Now Hannah, she spake in her heart; only her lips moved, but her voice was not heard: therefore Eli thought she had been drunken.* **14** *And Eli said unto her, How long wilt thou be drunken? put away thy wine from thee.*

Eli was the high priest of Israel in those days. He was the man of God. He saw Hannah bowing and moving her lips, but he did not hear a word from her. Apparently, people in those days were in the habit of praying out loud. Because Hannah was doing something a bit different, Eli jumped to the assumption that she was drunk. He actually accused her of that point-blank.

The problem is, he was wrong.

Any human being has the capacity to be utterly, completely wrong, including a man of God. That being the case, not one person in the ranks of humanity should ever be so foolish as to make assumptions!

DO develop the simple habit of asking questions before you assume anything. Unless, of course, you enjoy making yourself look like a donkey over and over again. If that is the case, by all means, continue to make assumptions.

Personal Notes:

_____

_____

_____

_____

_____

_____

_____

_____

_____

_____

_____

_____

_____

_____

_____

_____

_____

_____

_____

_____

_____

_____

_____

_____

_____

_____

_____

Devotion 36

Eli had made an assumption about Hannah, an assumption that turned out to be completely wrong. He accused her of being drunk. Here was her response to him:

1 Samuel 1:15 *And Hannah answered and said, No, my lord, I am a woman of a sorrowful spirit: I have drunk neither wine nor strong drink, but have poured out my soul before the LORD.* **16** *Count not thine handmaid for a daughter of Belial: for out of the abundance of my complaint and grief have I spoken hitherto.*

I am struck by the words of Hannah, not in that she defended herself, but in her very accurate view of how wicked it would have been had she actually been drunk as Eli accused. In our world today, drunkenness is a joke, a plot in sitcoms, a game at parties, just no big deal. But in Hannah's words, for her to have been drunk would have made her a "daughter of Belial." Belial means "worthlessness." In other words, being a drunk would have made her a "good for nothing."

Oh, how I wish that view would be reestablished in our modern world! Alcohol as a beverage ought to be a hated and despised abhorred thing among Christians, for no one ever got drunk without putting the bottle to their lips for the first time. As a pastor, I have seen very many homes wrecked by alcohol but not a single one ever improved by it!

DO take the same view of drunkenness that Hannah took. In order to avoid ever becoming a drunk, determine to do the one and only thing that is

100% successful at avoiding it; never drink alcohol at all.

Personal Notes:

_____

_____

_____

_____

_____

_____

_____

_____

_____

_____

_____

_____

_____

_____

_____

_____

_____

_____

_____

_____

_____

_____

_____

_____

_____

_____

_____

_____

_____

Devotion 37

Eli, the priest, had accused Hannah of being drunk as she prayed before the Lord. Hannah explained that she was not drunk at all; she was pouring out her grief before the Lord. Realizing the mistake that he had made, Eli then spoke much kinder and more sensible words to Hannah:

1 Samuel 1:17 *Then Eli answered and said, Go in peace: and the God of Israel grant thee thy petition that thou hast asked of him.*

Now please pay attention. As of this verse, absolutely nothing circumstance-wise had changed for Hannah. One verse earlier, she was barren, and in this verse, she was still barren. One verse earlier, she had no child, and in this verse, she had no child. And yet, look at her reaction to the words of Eli:

1 Samuel 1:18 *And she said, Let thine handmaid find grace in thy sight. So the woman went her way, and did eat, and her countenance was no more sad.*

Her countenance was no more sad. The look on her face had changed. She no longer appeared brokenhearted; she appeared happy. And yet her circumstances had not changed one iota.

Is it any wonder, Hannah, for thousands of years, has been regarded as a woman of faith? If we had read that she had a child and then her countenance was no more sad, there would be no faith in that whatsoever. Hannah believed before her circumstances ever changed.

DO be a man or woman of faith!

Personal Notes:

_____

_____

_____

_____

_____

_____

_____

_____

_____

_____

_____

_____

_____

_____

_____

_____

_____

_____

_____

_____

_____

_____

_____

_____

_____

_____

_____

_____

Devotion 38

Hannah had prayed, and based on the words of Eli, the high priest, she was quite certain that God was finally going to answer her prayer.

1 Samuel 1:19 *And they rose up in the morning early, and worshipped before the LORD, and returned, and came to their house to Ramah: and Elkanah knew Hannah his wife; and the LORD remembered her.* **20** *Wherefore it came to pass, when the time was come about after Hannah had conceived, that she bare a son, and called his name Samuel, saying, Because I have asked him of the LORD.*

Nine months or so pass in these two verses. The woman who had been childless and barren is now blessed with a baby boy. When he was born, she called his name Samuel. In her words, the reason she named him that was because she had "asked him of the Lord." His name was a reminder that he was an answer to prayer.

We know what this meant to Hannah, but consider what this meant to Samuel for the rest of his life! Day after day, until the day he died, his very name was a reminder to him that he owed his very existence to the God of heaven. What Hannah did was absolutely very good parenting.

What we name our children does not have to be directly from Scripture, that is not the point. The point is, from their earliest days, we should be inculcating them with a reverence for and gratitude toward the God of heaven.

DO, from the earliest days of your children, build that reverence for and gratitude toward God into them! When they have grown to know and love Him, you will be glad you did.

Personal Notes:

_____
_____
_____
_____
_____
_____
_____
_____
_____
_____
_____
_____
_____
_____
_____
_____
_____
_____
_____
_____
_____
_____
_____
_____
_____
_____
_____
_____
_____
_____
_____

Devotion 39

While barren and childless and praying in Shiloh, Hannah had made a promise that if God would give her a son, she would give him back to the Lord all the days of his life. That phrase may mean different things to different people, but to her, it meant that she would take him to live there in the Tabernacle so he could serve in the priesthood. You see, according to 1 Chronicles 6:33-38, the family of Samuel were Levites.

So, now Samuel had been born. And it is one thing to make a promise like the promise she made but quite another thing to carry it out. And yet listen to the words that we read from this dear new mother:

1 Samuel 1:21 *And the man Elkanah, and all his house, went up to offer unto the LORD the yearly sacrifice, and his vow.* **22** *But Hannah went not up; for she said unto her husband, I will not go up until the child be weaned, and then I will bring him, that he may appear before the LORD, and there abide for ever.*

Men were required to go to Shiloh each year; women were simply encouraged and allowed to do so. Normally, Hannah went each year with her husband. But this time around, she told him that she would not yet come; the child was not yet weaned, and the very next time she came with him, she intended to leave him there in the house of the Lord forever.

And she did.

DO "give your children to the Lord," parents. Samuel could have been a "good child" at home, but because his mother was selfless enough to give him to the Lord, he became one of the most important men Israel ever knew!

Personal Notes:

_____

_____

_____

_____

_____

_____

_____

_____

_____

_____

_____

_____

_____

_____

_____

_____

_____

_____

_____

_____

_____

_____

_____

_____

_____

_____

_____

_____

_____

_____

Devotion 40

In 1 Samuel 2, Hannah, who has now born a son and left him in the house of the Lord, opens her mouth, and the words began to pour forth. As the British family Bible notes point out, her words are actually a song. For ten verses, she prays and sings. But what is interesting is to compare some of her words with the words of another young lady many years later:

Luke 1:46 *And Mary said, My soul doth magnify the Lord,* **47** *And my spirit hath rejoiced in God my Saviour.* **48** *For he hath regarded the low estate of his handmaiden: for, behold, from henceforth all generations shall call me blessed.* **49** *For he that is mighty hath done to me great things; and holy is his name.*

These are just a few of the verses in what is commonly called the Magnificat. When you compare the content of Hannah's song to the content of Mary's song, you will find them incredibly similar.

At a time when Mary was facing her scariest moment because she was supernaturally having a child, she was able to look back in history and lean on the example of faith of another woman who had been supernaturally given a child by God. Yes, one was a human birth and one a divine birth, but both were supernatural.

Hannah obviously had no idea the impact she would have by simply praising the Lord. DO be in the habit of praising the Lord every single day; generations not even born yet may draw strength from what you do.

Personal Notes:

_____
_____
_____
_____
_____
_____
_____
_____
_____
_____
_____
_____
_____
_____
_____
_____
_____
_____
_____
_____
_____
_____
_____
_____
_____
_____
_____
_____

Devotion 41

As Hannah and Elkanah left little Samuel there in Shiloh and returned home, the scene began to shift away from them and back to the family of Eli. When that happened, an incredible juxtaposition is presented to us:

1 Samuel 2:11 *And Elkanah went to Ramah to his house. And the child did minister unto the LORD before Eli the priest.* **12** *Now the sons of Eli were sons of Belial; they knew not the LORD.*

Here we have two families on display. Family number one is just an average family who lives somewhere other than the Tabernacle. Family number two is the family of the high priest who lives in and around the Tabernacle every day of their lives. And yet the child of the first family was genuine, ministering to the Lord before Eli, the priest, while the two sons of Eli, the priest, were lost and wicked young men.

This ought to tell us that, as important as it is to be faithfully in the house of God, it is every bit as important and even more so that parents be godly and consistent in the home. We have already seen the godliness and consistency of Hannah and Elkanah; as the following chapters unfold, we will see the ungodliness and inconsistency of Eli. Their children are a predictable result of life in the home.

DO look at your home life and behavior, parents. If you are godly and consistent in the home, you will likely produce godly and consistent children. But if you are hypocrites, acting one way at church and then living another way at home, you will most likely produce reprobates.

Personal Notes:

_____

_____

_____

_____

_____

_____

_____

_____

_____

_____

_____

_____

_____

_____

_____

_____

_____

_____

_____

_____

_____

_____

_____

_____

_____

_____

_____

Devotion 42

In our last devotion, we looked at the juxtaposition between the family of Hannah and Elkanah and the family of Eli, the priest. We saw how their different lifestyles produced two radically different types of children.

That contrast is shown for us once again in the very same chapter. In 1 Samuel 2:12-16, we find the sons of Eli abusing both the sacrifices and the worshipers. They were even threatening violence on anyone who dared to say anything about it.

Having listed a great many of their iniquities, God then recorded another instance of how different these young men were:

1 Samuel 2:17 *Wherefore the sin of the young men was very great before the LORD: for men abhorred the offering of the LORD.* **18** *But Samuel ministered before the LORD, being a child, girded with a linen ephod.*

The sons of Eli, Hophni and Phinehas, were so incredibly wicked that people actually hated coming to the house of the Lord to worship just because of them. But Samuel, precious Samuel, just quietly and faithfully served the Lord even as a child. It would be Samuel who led the people to love the worship of the Lord, where Hophni and Phinehas made people hate it.

You who come to church, always remember that people, especially visitors, will either love the worship of the Lord or despise the worship of the Lord based largely on what they see from the people in God's house. DO wear a smile; DO be friendly; DO worship the Lord with all of your heart. Make people glad to come to God's house just because they know they will see you there!

Personal Notes:

_____

_____

_____

_____

_____

_____

_____

_____

_____

_____

_____

_____

_____

_____

_____

_____

_____

_____

_____

_____

_____

_____

_____

_____

_____

_____

_____

_____

_____

_____

Devotion 43

From the time he was just a child, Samuel was growing up in the house of the Lord, serving. His mother honored her vow to give him to the Lord forever. It surely must have been difficult to leave him there, but she did. However, she did not just "move on with life without him," she remained fully invested in the process in every way that she could.

1 Samuel 2:19 *Moreover his mother made him a little coat, and brought it to him from year to year, when she came up with her husband to offer the yearly sacrifice.*

She made him a little coat each year. With loving hands, she spun and wove the fabric, and each year that they came up to worship, she had him a new coat. Each one would of necessity be just a bit bigger than the year before. Each year of his growth, therefore, required a bit more effort from her.

And is that not exactly the way it is with our own children? As they grow stronger and more independent, it would seem like they would require less effort from us, but the exact opposite turns out to be true. The wise parent, especially when it comes to prayer and counsel, "makes the coat a bit bigger every year."

Parents, DO pray more for your children and counsel them more each year that they grow. Don't hover and smother, but DO make the coat just a bit bigger each year!

Personal Notes:

_____
_____
_____
_____
_____
_____
_____
_____
_____
_____
_____
_____
_____
_____
_____
_____
_____
_____
_____
_____
_____
_____
_____
_____
_____
_____

Devotion 44

When Eli had first noticed Hannah silently praying in Shiloh, he caustically assumed that she was drunk. But when she told him what was really going on, he quickly backtracked and said, "Go in peace: and the God of Israel grant thee thy petition that thou hast asked of him." Little did he know that meant she would one day be bringing her precious son to the house of the Lord and leaving him there forever to serve!

Samuel turned out to be a huge blessing to Eli. And because of that, one year there was another exchange between Hannah and him:

1 Samuel 2:20 *And Eli blessed Elkanah and his wife, and said, The LORD give thee seed of this woman for the loan which is lent to the LORD. And they went unto their own home.*

She had left her precious child there at Shiloh. Eli prayed that God would give her even more. And He did:

1 Samuel 2:21 *And the LORD visited Hannah, so that she conceived, and bare three sons and two daughters. And the child Samuel grew before the LORD.*

Hannah honored her vow and gave Samuel to the Lord. Her reward was both that she had five more children and that Samuel "grew before the Lord." God is not in the habit of being a debtor!

DO rest assured that God is aware of everything we give, and in terms of blessings, He always gives more in return!

Personal Notes:

_____

_____

_____

_____

_____

_____

_____

_____

_____

_____

_____

_____

_____

_____

_____

_____

_____

_____

_____

_____

_____

_____

_____

_____

_____

_____

_____

_____

_____

_____

Devotion 45

Samuel was growing, but the family of Eli was still in charge. And their ministry as priests was not a good thing:

1 Samuel 2:22 *Now Eli was very old, and heard all that his sons did unto all Israel; and how they lay with the women that assembled at the door of the tabernacle of the congregation.* **23** *And he said unto them, Why do ye such things? for I hear of your evil dealings by all this people.* **24** *Nay, my sons; for it is no good report that I hear: ye make the LORD'S people to transgress.*

Hophni and Phinehas were so wicked that they were committing both fornication and adultery (we later find that at least Phinehas was married!) right there at the very door of the tabernacle. These boys were horrible, and they were also still employed as priests. Their father Eli, the high priest, the one who could have put them out of the priesthood, the one who was, in fact, according to the law supposed to oversee them being stoned to death, "spoke to them" about the problem.

As we will later see, God expected much more than "speaking to them."

Parents, DO remember that sometimes words are simply not enough! The concept of punishment, especially corporal punishment, is viewed with horror in our world today but is still Biblical, effective, and necessary.

Personal Notes:

_____
_____
_____
_____
_____
_____
_____
_____
_____
_____
_____
_____
_____
_____
_____
_____
_____
_____
_____
_____
_____
_____
_____
_____
_____

Devotion 46

Samuel continued to grow up in the house of the Lord. As he grew, God had this to say of him:

1 Samuel 2:26 *And the child Samuel grew on, and was in favour both with the LORD, and also with men.*

Samuel behaved himself in such a way that both God and man had a high regard for him. The significant thing about that is the fact that he did so in the midst of horrible wickedness! The other "kids in the youth group" were fornicating right there in the house of God, abusing other worshipers, taking what did not belong to them, and their father just shrugged his shoulders and did nothing.

Samuel was not godly because of the crowd around him; he was godly in spite of the crowd around him.

Oftentimes people make excuses for their behavior, and those excuses can be encapsulated in the phrase "that's just the way things are now." Samuel did not care how things were; he only cared about how things were supposed to be.

DO determine, young or old, to live right before God and man no matter what anyone and everyone else around you is doing. People have to be reminded of the names Hophni and Phinehas, but people today are still naming their boys Samuel!

Personal Notes:

Devotion 47

It was the sons of Eli who were committing the actual wickedness and violence at the tabernacle, but it was Eli whom God held responsible. But what was anyone supposed to do? After all, Eli was the high priest; no one in the nation had more authority than he did.

But one unnamed man of God did not particularly care how powerful Eli and his family were:

1 Samuel 2:27 *And there came a man of God unto Eli, and said unto him, Thus saith the LORD, Did I plainly appear unto the house of thy father, when they were in Egypt in Pharaoh's house?*

All the way through verse thirty-six, this unnamed man of God delivers a message of doom to Eli. Without so much as flinching in the face of authority and power, he declared that God would kill both the sons of Eli, put an end to the house of Eli, and raise up a different priest.

This man was a hero. What he did could have cost him his life, but he did what needed to be done anyway. It has been rightly said, "Courage is not the absence of fear; it is doing what needs to be done in spite of your fear." These days not much is scarier than speaking the truth about wickedness. But it needed to be done then, and it needs to be done now.

DO be willing to follow God's leading, even when it is frightening to do so. This man may be unknown to us, but God thought so much of his courage that he sent him on a hero's mission!

Personal Notes:

_____

_____

_____

_____

_____

_____

_____

_____

_____

_____

_____

_____

_____

_____

_____

_____

_____

_____

_____

_____

_____

_____

_____

_____

_____

_____

Devotion 48

As we enter into 1 Samuel 3, we are given a commentary that is both wonderful and sad all at the same time.

1 Samuel 3:1 *And the child Samuel ministered unto the LORD before Eli. And the word of the LORD was precious in those days; there was no open vision.*

In those days, there was no "open vision." In other words, there was no publically recognized prophet being given any word from the Lord to give to the people. No one was saying, "Thus saith the Lord," because the Lord was not saying much. The sin of the people had made Him cease to give His word to them. Therefore, because there was not much "word of the Lord," what little bit they did have, written or spoken, was precious to them.

Do you see why that is both wonderful and sad? It took scarcity of the Word of God to make it precious to the people.

People around the world are clamoring for just one Bible, maybe even for just a part of a Bible. When they get it, they devour it. We walk from one end of our houses to the other and pass ten dusty Bibles along the way.

DO make the Word of God much more precious in your life. If we in America will treat it like the most precious thing we have, we will probably always have it. If we do not regard it as precious, one day we will look around and wonder how we as a society lost it altogether.

Personal Notes:

_____

_____

_____

_____

_____

_____

_____

_____

_____

_____

_____

_____

_____

_____

_____

_____

_____

_____

_____

_____

_____

_____

_____

_____

_____

_____

_____

_____

Devotion 49

Nighttime had fallen in Shiloh where the Tabernacle of God was. The sons of Eli were unaccounted for in this text, most likely out engaging in their habitual wickedness. Eli, the high priest, though, and young Samuel were inside the Tabernacle compound. And it is inside the Tabernacle that we find another subtle indication of the spiritual decay in the land:

1 Samuel 3:2 *And it came to pass at that time, when Eli was laid down in his place, and his eyes began to wax dim, that he could not see; 3 And ere the lamp of God went out in the temple of the LORD, where the ark of God was, and Samuel was laid down to sleep;*

The text mentions that what is about to take place took place before the lamp of God went out in the Tabernacle of the Lord, where the Ark of God was. The problem with that is that lamp was never supposed to go out to begin with:

Exodus 27:20 *And thou shalt command the children of Israel, that they bring thee pure oil olive beaten for the light, to cause the lamp to burn always.*

Always. The lamp was to burn always. But this required a great deal of work preparing the oil and tending to the lamp. So somewhere along the line Eli and his family decided that only keeping the lamp burning part-time would save them some effort; after all, only a tiny handful of people were ever allowed inside to see.

Little wonder that we see them cutting corners on every other matter of righteousness as well.

DO remember that the little things in our lives, often unseen by others, are good indicators of our spiritual condition. If we are not doing right on things unseen, we are probably not doing right on much at all!

Personal Notes:

_____

_____

_____

_____

_____

_____

_____

_____

_____

_____

_____

_____

_____

_____

_____

_____

_____

_____

_____

_____

_____

_____

_____

_____

_____

Devotion 50

In 1 Samuel 3:4-8, God began to speak to young Samuel in the Tabernacle by night. Each time He spoke, calling his name, Samuel assumed it was Eli calling him. The first two times that it happened, Eli sent him back to bed, saying, "I didn't call you." But the third time it happened, it dawned on Eli that God was speaking to Samuel. At that point, he gave Samuel this good instruction:

1 Samuel 3:9 *Therefore Eli said unto Samuel, Go, lie down: and it shall be, if he call thee, that thou shalt say, Speak, LORD; for thy servant heareth. So Samuel went and lay down in his place.*

Speak, Lord; for thy servant heareth. Eli was right; those were the proper words for Samuel to say. The problem was, he did not heed his own advice. God had spoken to Eli about the wickedness of his sons, and Eli had not responded as he should. Eli was giving Samuel all the right counsel with his mouth and ignoring that own counsel in his own life. That resulted in the destruction of him and his entire family.

Good advice is, well, good. Giving good advice is not the problem; giving good advice that we ourselves do not follow is the problem. DO tell others from Scripture the right way to go, the right things to do. But DO remember that the far more important thing is actually doing right yourself! Advice is cheap; action is priceless.

Personal Notes:

_____
_____
_____
_____
_____
_____
_____
_____
_____
_____
_____
_____
_____
_____
_____
_____
_____
_____
_____
_____
_____
_____
_____
_____

Devotion 51

The years of childhood quickly passed by for little Samuel. As he grew, his reputation in the land grew as well:

1 Samuel 3:19 *And Samuel grew, and the LORD was with him, and did let none of his words fall to the ground.* **20** *And all Israel from Dan even to Beersheba knew that Samuel was established to be a prophet of the LORD.* **21** *And the LORD appeared again in Shiloh: for the LORD revealed himself to Samuel in Shiloh by the word of the LORD.*

Everyone knew and understood that the Lord had appointed Samuel to be a prophet. Where the Word of God prior to the days of Samuel had been very scarce, there was now a man on the scene who could truthfully say the words, "Thus saith the Lord."

Concerning Samuel, this text uses an interesting phrase about him. It says that the Lord "let none of his words fall to the ground." That is a metaphor, which means that whatever he said came true. It is not that he had the power to speak something into existence, quite the opposite. The reason that whatever he said came true is because he only spoke the words of God.

Our authority as Christians in what we speak is never found in our opinions or intelligence or predictions. The only authority our words have is that they come from the Word of God. And if they do not come from the Word of God, they have no authority.

Every Christian, not just preachers, should consume and memorize vast quantities of Scripture on a regular basis. DO understand that if we are not speaking the Word of God, we may have passion, and we may be convinced of what we are saying, but we do not have any authority, any right to say, "This is true; this is the way things must be done!"

Personal Notes:

_____

_____

_____

_____

_____

_____

_____

_____

_____

_____

_____

_____

_____

_____

_____

_____

_____

_____

_____

_____

_____

_____

_____

_____

_____

_____

_____

_____

Devotion 52

1 Samuel 4 is the scene of a tragedy and an irony all at the same time.

1 Samuel 4:1 *And the word of Samuel came to all Israel. Now Israel went out against the Philistines to battle, and pitched beside Ebenezer: and the Philistines pitched in Aphek.* **2** *And the Philistines put themselves in array against Israel: and when they joined battle, Israel was smitten before the Philistines: and they slew of the army in the field about four thousand men.* **3a** *And when the people were come into the camp, the elders of Israel said, Wherefore hath the LORD smitten us to day before the Philistines?*

Four thousand men died in the battle. When that happened, the elders of Israel, the people in charge, the people who were supposed to have the answers said, "Why has God done this?"

Apparently, they were the only people in the entire nation who did not know the answer. Remember that everyone in the nation hated coming to the house of God to worship because of the behavior of Eli's family!

Ignorance does not pay, especially ignorance in matters of unspiritual behavior. Every one of us has a responsibility to know what God expects, and to do what God expects!

DO evaluate your life carefully and regularly through the lens of Scripture. If there are changes that need to be made, make them before the tragedy falls, before people who should know better are asking the question, "Why has God done this?"

Personal Notes:

_____

_____

_____

_____

_____

_____

_____

_____

_____

_____

_____

_____

_____

_____

_____

_____

_____

_____

_____

_____

_____

_____

_____

_____

_____

_____

Devotion 53

Four thousand men were dead in the battle versus the Philistines. The elders of Israel were frantically asking, "Why has God done this? Why has He let us lose the battle? Why did He let so many people die?"

That would have been an excellent time to stop everything, find the problem, and get it right before going back to battle. But instead, they made the most horrible, unthinkable decision imaginable:

1 Samuel 4:3 *And when the people were come into the camp, the elders of Israel said, Wherefore hath the LORD smitten us to day before the Philistines? Let us fetch the ark of the covenant of the LORD out of Shiloh unto us, that, when it cometh among us, it may save us out of the hand of our enemies.*

They "fetched" the Ark of the Covenant so that "it" could save them. I understand that the word "fetched" did not to them bring to mind the picture of a drooling dog chasing a meaningless stick and bringing it back as it does to us, but their thought process on it was just about as bad as that. They regarded the Ark of God as some kind of a magic box that they could drag around to do their bidding. Rather than trusting a "Him," they put their faith in an "it," a box, understanding neither the significance of the Ark nor of the God who gave it to them.

DO understand the significance of holy things (the Bible, church, etc.) and the God who gave them to us. Our "its" are only precious when we understand their connection to "Him!"

Personal Notes:

_____

_____

_____

_____

_____

_____

_____

_____

_____

_____

_____

_____

_____

_____

_____

_____

_____

_____

_____

_____

_____

_____

_____

_____

_____

_____

_____

_____

Devotion 54

The Children of Israel made the horrible mistake of assuming that God would save them from the Philistines just because they brought the Ark of the Covenant to the battlefield:

1 Samuel 4:4 *So the people sent to Shiloh, that they might bring from thence the ark of the covenant of the LORD of hosts, which dwelleth between the cherubims: and the two sons of Eli, Hophni and Phinehas, were there with the ark of the covenant of God. 5 And when the ark of the covenant of the LORD came into the camp, all Israel shouted with a great shout, so that the earth rang again.*

The Ark had been residing in Shiloh for many years. Now the priests, the caretakers of the Ark, allowed it to be removed from Shiloh and brought to the battlefield. We will see in succeeding verses how that plan did not work, and Israel suffered a great defeat in spite of the presence of the Ark of the Covenant. But for now, what we really need to focus on is this one fact: we never again in Scripture read of the Ark of God making it back to Shiloh.

So very often, we allow precious things to slip away, assuming we can always easily get them back, things like a good reputation, a close walk with God, a good relationship with people who are precious to us, and many more. But if we treat things that are precious in a careless manner, just like the Children of Israel, we may find out that we never get them back.

DO take stock of those things and people that are precious to you and treat them accordingly!

Personal Notes:

_____
_____
_____
_____
_____
_____
_____
_____
_____
_____
_____
_____
_____
_____
_____
_____
_____
_____
_____
_____
_____
_____
_____
_____
_____
_____
_____
_____
_____

Devotion 55

The children of Israel had done the most unthinkable of things; they brought the Ark of the Covenant out of Shiloh to the battlefield against the Philistines. They were counting on it to give them victory, but they quickly found that would not be the case:

1 Samuel 4:10 *And the Philistines fought, and Israel was smitten, and they fled every man into his tent: and there was a very great slaughter; for there fell of Israel thirty thousand footmen.* **11** *And the ark of God was taken; and the two sons of Eli, Hophni and Phinehas, were slain.*

Thirty thousand men dead. The Ark of God taken. The two sons of Eli slain. Things could not have turned out much worse at all.

But remember that the problem that caused it all was not an "out there" problem; it was an "in here" problem. Things were not right in the house of God, and that very specifically is the reason all of this disaster took place.

That is a sobering warning for today, don't you think? When you consider things like unfaithfulness and unholiness and prayerlessness, it is evident that the church of today has its own issues to deal with!

DO realize that what happens in the world largely depends on what happens in church, and what happens in the church depends on you!

Personal Notes:

_____

_____

_____

_____

_____

_____

_____

_____

_____

_____

_____

_____

_____

_____

_____

_____

_____

_____

_____

_____

_____

_____

_____

_____

_____

_____

_____

_____

Devotion 56

After the slaughter at the hands of the Philistines, a messenger came running back into the camp and gave Eli all the bad news. When Eli heard that the Ark of God had been taken, he fell backward off of his stool, broke his neck, and died.

But as if things were not bad enough, the wife of Phinehas, one of Eli's sons that had just died, was at that moment greatly pregnant, and when she heard all of the bad news, she went into labor and died shortly after having given birth.

But just before she died, she named the child, and his name had a very significant meaning:

1 Samuel 4:21 *And she named the child Ichabod, saying, The glory is departed from Israel: because the ark of God was taken, and because of her father in law and her husband.*

Ichabod. The glory is departed. She gave him this name because the Ark of God was taken. But you see, the Ark of God, while the most sacred piece of furniture Israel had ever been given, was not actually the glory of God; it was just the place where the glory of God visibly rested. The real glory of God was in all that He had done for His people and in the close relationship that they once had with Him! And that had been gone for a very long time.

DO realize that the real glory of God for us, His people, will never be in symbols or in structures. Our glory will forever be in having a close walk with the God who has saved us. If we maintain that, no other loss can ever take the glory from us!

Personal Notes:

_____
_____
_____
_____
_____
_____
_____
_____
_____
_____
_____
_____
_____
_____
_____
_____
_____
_____
_____
_____
_____
_____
_____
_____
_____
_____

Devotion 57

To say that capturing the Ark of God was a surprise to the Philistines would be the understatement of the century. They never dreamed it would ever be brought out to the battlefield to begin with, much less that they could capture it. So, when they did capture it, they quickly had to figure out something to do with it. What they did and the result that came from it is, in many ways, hysterical.

1 Samuel 5:1 *And the Philistines took the ark of God, and brought it from Ebenezer unto Ashdod.* **2** *When the Philistines took the ark of God, they brought it into the house of Dagon, and set it by Dagon.* **3** *And when they of Ashdod arose early on the morrow, behold, Dagon was fallen upon his face to the earth before the ark of the LORD. And they took Dagon, and set him in his place again.*

Dagon was one of the deities of the Philistines, a half-fish/half-man idol carved by human beings and standing erect in their temple. The Philistines put the Ark of God by Dagon, and the next morning Dagon was bowing before it! The fun was only beginning on that, there would be more to come, but for now, let's just focus on the fact that a false god was bowing before the Ark of the real God.

If an idol, not even an animate thing, feels compelled to bow before the Lord of glory, how much more can we be assured that one day every knee will bow to Christ!

DO rejoice in the fact that you bow the knee willingly now, and also in the fact that one day you will be able to observe every knee bow to the King!

Personal Notes:

Devotion 58

After the Philistines found Dagon bowing before the Ark of the Covenant, they set it back up its place. But the next morning, things got exponentially worse for them:

1 Samuel 5:4 *And when they arose early on the morrow morning, behold, Dagon was fallen upon his face to the ground before the ark of the LORD; and the head of Dagon and both the palms of his hands were cut off upon the threshold; only the stump of Dagon was left to him.* **5** *Therefore neither the priests of Dagon, nor any that come into Dagon's house, tread on the threshold of Dagon in Ashdod unto this day.*

It is clear that no one among the Philistines would do such a thing, nor could anyone among the Israelites get in that place to do such a thing. The Philistines knew, therefore, that the God of the Hebrews had done this. To see the head and hands cut off of their deity and laying upon the threshold was such a shock to their system that when Samuel wrote this account down many years later he made a note of the fact that to that day no one would even walk on the spot where it happened!

God has a great way of getting a point across, don't you think?

Idolatry is foolishness; it always has been. Who in their right mind worships a "god" that they can make with their hands? This was the chief difference between Dagon and the Ark. Dagon was a deity to the Philistines; the Ark was merely a place for the living God to rest upon and make Himself known.

DO be encouraged by the fact that your God
was not made by you; your God made you!

Personal Notes:

_____

_____

_____

_____

_____

_____

_____

_____

_____

_____

_____

_____

_____

_____

_____

_____

_____

_____

_____

_____

_____

_____

_____

_____

_____

_____

_____

Devotion 59

It was becoming clearer and clearer to the Philistines that they did not know what they had gotten ahold of when they took the Ark from Israel. The next thing we read in the account shows God once again making the Philistines regret ever having taken the Ark:

1 Samuel 5:6 *But the hand of the LORD was heavy upon them of Ashdod, and he destroyed them, and smote them with emerods, even Ashdod and the coasts thereof. 7 And when the men of Ashdod saw that it was so, they said, The ark of the God of Israel shall not abide with us: for his hand is sore upon us, and upon Dagon our god.*

You probably do not recognize the painful humor found in this passage. But when you know the definition of one of the odd words in it, it will become very clear. "Emerods" is an old English word for hemorrhoids.

Ouch. Just ouch. To say that God "hit them where it hurt" would be quite the understatement. These people could not get rid of the Ark fast enough! Israel may have been disobedient to God, but at least they were His people. God was making it very plain to the Philistines that there was a difference between them and the Hebrews.

On our worst days, on the days when we stumble and fall and slip and feel miserable, DO remember that we, the saved, are the people of God, and God always looks at us differently than He does the lost!

Personal Notes:

Devotion 60

Dagon had been smitten, the Philistines had gotten hemorrhoids, and many of them had been slain. They wanted to keep the Ark; it was their greatest battle trophy. But what they wanted even more was for the pain to go away!

1 Samuel 6:1 *And the ark of the LORD was in the country of the Philistines seven months.* **2** *And the Philistines called for the priests and the diviners, saying, What shall we do to the ark of the LORD? tell us wherewith we shall send it to his place.* **3** *And they said, If ye send away the ark of the God of Israel, send it not empty; but in any wise return him a trespass offering: then ye shall be healed, and it shall be known to you why his hand is not removed from you.*

The Philistines made known the fact that after seven months with the Ark in their land, things were not getting better; the judging hand of the God of the Hebrews had not been removed from them.

Seven months. Seven months of hemorrhoids and death and their idols being smitten. To quote the younger folk's vernacular today, "Stubborn, much?"

DO learn a lesson from these hard-headed Philistines. God can swing the paddle for a very long time without getting the least bit tired or even breaking a sweat. It is an excellent idea to obey Him and do right rather than try to wait for Him to get tired of swinging that paddle!

Personal Notes:

_____
_____
_____
_____
_____
_____
_____
_____
_____
_____
_____
_____
_____
_____
_____
_____
_____
_____
_____
_____
_____
_____
_____
_____
_____
_____
_____

Devotion 61

The Philistines were in quite a mess. For seven months, they had been experiencing the heavy hand of God in judgment upon them for having the Ark of God. Finally, it had gotten bad enough that they determined to send it back to Israel. But when they asked how they should do so, the answer that they received from their Philistine counselors contained a very unique insight:

1 Samuel 6:4 *Then said they, What shall be the trespass offering which we shall return to him? They answered, Five golden emerods, and five golden mice, according to the number of the lords of the Philistines: for one plague was on you all, and on your lords.* **5** *Wherefore ye shall make images of your emerods, and images of your mice that mar the land; and ye shall give glory unto the God of Israel: peradventure he will lighten his hand from off you, and from off your gods, and from off your land.* **6** *Wherefore then do ye harden your hearts, as the Egyptians and Pharaoh hardened their hearts? when he had wrought wonderfully among them, did they not let the people go, and they departed?*

Notice that in verse six, their priests and diviners chastised them for hardening their hearts just as the Egyptians had done. From the words they used, it is evident that there were those among the Philistines who, despite the death and destruction God was visiting upon them, did not want to let the Ark of God go. These counselors of the Philistines pointed back in time about 500 years to the judgments upon Egypt and the exodus.

Do you realize what they, therefore, clearly understood? They understood that the real God never changes.

DO rejoice in knowing that the God you serve is the same God of Abraham, Moses, David, Peter, and Paul. He is the same God of all power that He has always been, and we can rest in His strength every day of our lives!

Personal Notes:

_____

_____

_____

_____

_____

_____

_____

_____

_____

_____

_____

_____

_____

_____

_____

_____

_____

_____

_____

_____

_____

_____

Devotion 62

The Philistines finally sent the Ark of God back to the land of Israel. They had no clue what to do with it, and many of them ended up dead because of it. But when it got back to the land of Israel, we find out that, sadly, the Israelites seemingly had no more clue what to do with it than the heathen Philistines:

1 Samuel 6:19 *And he smote the men of Bethshemesh, because they had looked into the ark of the LORD, even he smote of the people fifty thousand and threescore and ten men: and the people lamented, because the LORD had smitten many of the people with a great slaughter.* **20** *And the men of Bethshemesh said, Who is able to stand before this holy LORD God? and to whom shall he go up from us?* **21** *And they sent messengers to the inhabitants of Kirjathjearim, saying, The Philistines have brought again the ark of the LORD; come ye down, and fetch it up to you.*

More than fifty thousand people, dead, smitten by God, for trying to do the most forbidden thing in Jewish life, trying to look into the Ark of the Covenant!

Not trying to make light of anything, but even Indiana Jones knew better than that. And yet, the people who should have known it better than anyone did not.

DO understand how vital it is that we not only know the truth of God in Scripture but that we pass it down to our children and grandchildren. Somewhere along the line in Israel, people stopped communicating the truth about the Ark of God and the

God of the Ark, and that oversight led to a great many people paying the price with their lives.

Personal Notes:

_____

_____

_____

_____

_____

_____

_____

_____

_____

_____

_____

_____

_____

_____

_____

_____

_____

_____

_____

_____

_____

_____

_____

_____

_____

_____

_____

Devotion 63

The Ark of God finally found a resting place back home in Israel and for a comparatively long period of time:

1 Samuel 7:1 *And the men of Kirjathjearim came, and fetched up the ark of the LORD, and brought it into the house of Abinadab in the hill, and sanctified Eleazar his son to keep the ark of the LORD. 2 And it came to pass, while the Ark abode in Kirjathjearim, that the time was long; for it was twenty years: and all the house of Israel lamented after the LORD.*

For twenty years, the Bible tells us that all the house of Israel lamented after the Lord. They were crying and weeping because, in their view, the Lord had abandoned Israel and was nowhere to be found. Mind you, the Ark was actually there for a great deal longer than that as we will see in succeeding chapters, but it was there for twenty years before they finally got serious enough about their sin to repent as we see in verses three and following.

But for every day of those same twenty years, there was one dedicated, faithful man who knew that the Lord had not abandoned Israel, Eleazar, the son of Abinadab. The reason he knew that God had not abandoned Israel was that every single day, he was personally meeting with God! For twenty years, he tended to the very Ark of God.

DO know that no matter how many people, due to their sin, decide that God is simply no longer around, each one of us has the option of living right and meeting with Him individually on a daily basis regardless of what the rest of the world may do! God

RULES nations, but He FELLOWSHIPS with individuals!

Personal Notes:

_____

_____

_____

_____

_____

_____

_____

_____

_____

_____

_____

_____

_____

_____

_____

_____

_____

_____

_____

_____

_____

_____

_____

_____

_____

_____

Devotion 64

After twenty years of, in their view, being without God, the people were finally ready to have a finger put on their very specific sins that were separating between them and their God.

1 Samuel 7:3 *And Samuel spake unto all the house of Israel, saying, If ye do return unto the LORD with all your hearts, then put away the strange gods and Ashtaroth from among you, and prepare your hearts unto the LORD, and serve him only: and he will deliver you out of the hand of the Philistines.* **4** *Then the children of Israel did put away Baalim and Ashtaroth, and served the LORD only.*

Idolatry was ever the Achilles' heel of the children of Israel. But as we study their history, very rarely, if ever, did they forsake God entirely. They did something that was actually worse; they lumped Him in with other false gods and "served" all of them. This was the exact same problem they had in the days of Elijah when he had to ask them, "How long halt ye between two opinions?"

As horrible as it is not to love and serve the one true God, it is even worse to act as if He is simply one among many gods.

DO remember that our God is Who and What He says He is; He is God ALONE and must be worshiped as such!

Personal Notes:

Devotion 65

The children of Israel were finally broken to the point that they were willing to serve the Lord only. They had repented. But look, please, at the very next thing that happened.

1 Samuel 7:4 *Then the children of Israel did put away Baalim and Ashtaroth, and served the LORD only.* **5** *And Samuel said, Gather all Israel to Mizpeh, and I will pray for you unto the LORD.* **6** *And they gathered together to Mizpeh, and drew water, and poured it out before the LORD, and fasted on that day, and said there, We have sinned against the LORD. And Samuel judged the children of Israel in Mizpeh.* **7** *And when the Philistines heard that the children of Israel were gathered together to Mizpeh, the lords of the Philistines went up against Israel. And when the children of Israel heard it, they were afraid of the Philistines.*

They got right with God…and the very next thing that happened was that they were attacked and found themselves in a fight for their survival!

People often assume that when they get saved or get right with God, things will get easier. But what they often get is the exact opposite! You see, when people finally enter into a right relationship with God, the devil becomes their immediate and very active enemy. But what that tells us is that if the devil is fighting us, we are actually on the right side for a change!

DO pray for good days and peace, but when the hard days come as a result of being right with God, rejoice in the fact that having the right enemy means you are on the righ side!

Personal Notes:

_____
_____
_____
_____
_____
_____
_____
_____
_____
_____
_____
_____
_____
_____
_____
_____
_____
_____
_____
_____
_____
_____
_____
_____
_____

Devotion 66

The children of Israel had gotten right with God, and immediately the Philistines had come out to battle against them. Twenty years earlier when the Philistines had come against them, they made the most horrible mistake imaginable, taking the Ark of God out onto the battlefield.

What would they do this time?

1 Samuel 7:8 *And the children of Israel said to Samuel, Cease not to cry unto the LORD our God for us, that he will save us out of the hand of the Philistines.* **9** *And Samuel took a sucking lamb, and offered it for a burnt offering wholly unto the LORD: and Samuel cried unto the LORD for Israel; and the LORD heard him.* **10** *And as Samuel was offering up the burnt offering, the Philistines drew near to battle against Israel: but the LORD thundered with a great thunder on that day upon the Philistines, and discomfited them; and they were smitten before Israel.*

They prayed, they worshiped, they fought, and God gave a great victory. What they did not do was repeat the mistakes of the past! Remember that they knew exactly where the Ark of God was, they had easy access to it, but they did not go after it this time. Give them credit for having learned their lesson!

Experience is a hard teacher. DO learn the lessons that it teaches quickly and preferably without having to have those lessons repeated!

Personal Notes:

_____
_____
_____
_____
_____
_____
_____
_____
_____
_____
_____
_____
_____
_____
_____
_____
_____
_____
_____
_____
_____
_____
_____
_____
_____
_____

Devotion 67

When Samuel had been just a little boy, the nation of Israel had been in a mess for one specific reason: Eli, the priest, allowed his sons to be in positions of authority when those boys were wicked and ungodly men. In that horrible environment, God raised up little Samuel to change everything.

And that is what makes what we read in the following verses such a sad and utterly surprising thing.

1 Samuel 8:1 *And it came to pass, when Samuel was old, that he made his sons judges over Israel.* **2** *Now the name of his firstborn was Joel; and the name of his second, Abiah: they were judges in Beersheba.* **3** *And his sons walked not in his ways, but turned aside after lucre, and took bribes, and perverted judgment.*

Samuel and his sons ended up looking like a remake of a movie of Eli and his sons!

Bear in mind that the boys being wicked was not the ultimate problem. It is entirely possible for parents to be godly and do everything right and still have a child or children turn out bad; just consider the account of the prodigal son as proof of that.

The real problem, therefore, was that Samuel put his sons in positions of authority, even knowing what they were like. He chose family over godliness; he chose to make the good of the nation secondary to doing something "nice" for his unworthy children.

DO understand that anyone's children can go bad. If and when they do, it is perfectly acceptable to still love them, but it is never acceptable to give unrighteous people positions and benefits that should only be given to righteous people!

Personal Notes:

_____
_____
_____
_____
_____
_____
_____
_____
_____
_____
_____
_____
_____
_____
_____
_____
_____
_____
_____
_____
_____
_____
_____
_____
_____
_____
_____

Devotion 68

The wickedness of the sons of Samuel gave the children of Israel the excuse they needed to ask for something that they were not truly ready to have.

1 Samuel 8:4 *Then all the elders of Israel gathered themselves together, and came to Samuel unto Ramah,* **5** *And said unto him, Behold, thou art old, and thy sons walk not in thy ways: now make us a king to judge us like all the nations.* **6** *But the thing displeased Samuel, when they said, Give us a king to judge us. And Samuel prayed unto the LORD.* **7** *And the LORD said unto Samuel, Hearken unto the voice of the people in all that they say unto thee: for they have not rejected thee, but they have rejected me, that I should not reign over them.*

Though the Israelites couched their demand for a king at least partially under the guise of trying to be free from the wickedness of the sons of Samuel, God saw through that excuse. He told Samuel, who was incredibly upset over the entire ordeal, that the children of Israel had not rejected him but, in reality, had rejected God.

In other words, God told Samuel not to take it personally. Their grievance was not really against him; their grievance was against God.

Oftentimes we as Christians will find people, in our view, rejecting us and pushing us away for the truths that we speak. Whenever that happens, DO take great comfort in the fact that even if they are fussing at you, they are really angry with God. So sleep peaceably and remember that as long as you are right with God, it is not really that big of a deal if others are "wrong with you!"

Personal Notes:

_____
_____
_____
_____
_____
_____
_____
_____
_____
_____
_____
_____
_____
_____
_____
_____
_____
_____
_____
_____
_____
_____
_____
_____
_____
_____
_____
_____

Devotion 69

The children of Israel had demanded a king. In 1 Samuel 8:11-18, Samuel laid out exactly what they were in for if they got their way. The list was long and brutal; people thinking clearly would never have chosen to go that way.

Nevertheless, Israel was determined to have their way on this:

1 Samuel 8:19 *Nevertheless the people refused to obey the voice of Samuel; and they said, Nay; but we will have a king over us; 20 That we also may be like all the nations; and that our king may judge us, and go out before us, and fight our battles.*

We see in verse twenty that their motivation for what they were asking was so that they could "be like all the nations." This was an excellent case of "the grass is always greener on the other side of the fence."

But since they were determined, God told Samuel to give them their way:

1 Samuel 8:22a *And the LORD said to Samuel, Hearken unto their voice, and make them a king.*

In very short order, they would have their first king. And three kings after that they would have a Civil War that irrevocably split the nation and led to the eventual downfall of both sides. It was a very short trip from "getting their way" to "wishing they hadn't."

DO remember that if you push hard enough, God may very well give you your way, and if that ever happens, you will inevitably reach a point where you wish that He hadn't!

Personal Notes:

_____
_____
_____
_____
_____
_____
_____
_____
_____
_____
_____
_____
_____
_____
_____
_____
_____
_____
_____
_____
_____
_____
_____
_____
_____
_____

Devotion 70

Having badgered God to the point where He agreed to give them a king, 2 Samuel 9 gives us the introductory remarks about the man who was to become that king.

1 Samuel 9:1 *Now there was a man of Benjamin, whose name was Kish, the son of Abiel, the son of Zeror, the son of Bechorath, the son of Aphiah, a Benjamite, a mighty man of power.* **2** *And he had a son, whose name was Saul, a choice young man, and a goodly: and there was not among the children of Israel a goodlier person than he: from his shoulders and upward he was higher than any of the people.*

We are told here that Saul was "goodly." In fact, the very next phrase tells us that no one in the entire nation was "a goodlier person than he." That word goodly refers to the fact that he was physically attractive. Saul, quite literally, was the most attractive man in the entire country. But in the very next phrase, we also find that he was the tallest man in the entire country!

It is safe to say that Saul was the greatest physical specimen to ever sit on the throne of the king of Israel. He could have gone from the battlefield to the cover of a magazine to the red carpet of Hollywood and been well received in every place.

But do you notice the glaring omission in the description of him? Not one thing is said about Saul being a spiritual man. All Israel saw was the physical, the omission of the spiritual was going to cost them dearly.

DO make your chief evaluations of people spiritual evaluations rather than physical evaluations.

142

No one is ever attractive enough to make up for lack of godliness!

Personal Notes:

_____

_____

_____

_____

_____

_____

_____

_____

_____

_____

_____

_____

_____

_____

_____

_____

_____

_____

_____

_____

_____

_____

_____

_____

_____

Devotion 71

In 1 Samuel 9:3, Kish, the father of Saul, came up missing some donkeys. So he sent his son and a servant looking for them:

1 Samuel 9:3 *And the asses of Kish Saul's father were lost. And Kish said to Saul his son, Take now one of the servants with thee, and arise, go seek the asses.*

Verses four and five describe the very long trek that these two men took trying to find the donkeys, all to no avail. And so at the end of verse five, Saul told his servant that they should return home because his father was going to end up more worried about their absence than any missing donkeys. The servant, though, had another suggestion. And it is in that suggestion that we find something both wonderful and heartbreaking all at once.

1 Samuel 9:6 *And he said unto him, Behold now, there is in this city a man of God, and he is an honourable man; all that he saith cometh surely to pass: now let us go thither; peradventure he can shew us our way that we should go.*

Pay attention to that phrase, "there is in this city a man of God, and he is an honorable man."

Do you see why that is both wonderful and heartbreaking? It is wonderful that the man of God, Samuel in this instance, was an honorable man and recognized as such. But it is heartbreaking that those words even needed to be uttered.

Not just for preachers but for every child of God, it ought to be incredibly redundant to refer to us as "honorable!" The horrible behavior of Eli and his sons, and then the sons of Samuel themselves, so marred the testimony of the ministry that this servant felt the need to clarify that this particular man of God was honorable, as opposed to others.

DO be honorable in every single thing you do, great or small, every single day. What you do as a child of God will either lower or raise the estimation of Christians in general in the eyes of everyone with whom you interact!

Personal Notes:

_____

_____

_____

_____

_____

_____

_____

_____

_____

_____

_____

_____

_____

_____

_____

_____

_____

_____

_____

Devotion 72

Saul and his servant made their way into the town where Samuel the prophet was. Samuel was actually expecting him. God had told him a day before that he would be coming, and Samuel was to anoint Saul as king. Saul knew absolutely none of this; he was just looking for missing donkeys! What he got was something far greater entirely:

1 Samuel 10:1 *Then Samuel took a vial of oil, and poured it upon his head, and kissed him, and said, Is it not because the LORD hath anointed thee to be captain over his inheritance?*

When he left home in obedience to his father searching for the donkeys, Saul had no idea he would come back home with the anointing of God upon him, chosen to be the first king of Israel. His greatness was not something that he sought for; it was something that got handed to him in the midst of simple, everyday obedience in small things.

So very often people want to be great, and they set about each and every day trying to make themselves a name. But real greatness, greatness given by God, always originates with humble and obedient hearts just willing to serve in small things.

DO seek after greatness in the sight of God, but DO pursue it by every single day being obedient to His will and serving Him in whatever often unseen and unheralded ways He lays before you!

Personal Notes:

_____

_____

_____

_____

_____

_____

_____

_____

_____

_____

_____

_____

_____

_____

_____

_____

_____

_____

_____

_____

_____

_____

_____

_____

_____

_____

_____

_____

_____

Devotion 73

After Samuel anointed Saul and told him that he would be the next king of Israel, he gave the clearly skeptical young man a series of signs in 1 Samuel 10:2-5 that he was to watch for, signs that would prove what Samuel was saying beyond a doubt.

But it is in verse six that Samuel said perhaps the most important words of all to the man who would be king:

1 Samuel 10:6 *And the Spirit of the LORD will come upon thee, and thou shalt prophesy with them, and shalt be turned into another man.*

Thou shalt be turned into another man. What a statement!

Understand that God is not looking through the ranks of humanity to find men and women and boys and girls who are already so special and amazing that He is simply compelled to use them. On the contrary; He is actually looking for people that He can radically transform into someone who will be useful!

Many days we will feel, as Saul did, somewhat useless. On those days take heart, and DO remember that, if you are in your mind "useless," you might be just what God is looking for, because when He makes a person "another man" or "another woman," He receives the glory for what they become and what they accomplish!

Personal Notes:

_____

_____

_____

_____

_____

_____

_____

_____

_____

_____

_____

_____

_____

_____

_____

_____

_____

_____

_____

_____

_____

_____

_____

_____

_____

_____

_____

_____

Devotion 74

Having anointed Saul to be the first king of Israel, the next task was to make all of the nation aware of it:

1 Samuel 10:17 *And Samuel called the people together unto the LORD to Mizpeh;*

Once Samuel had gathered them, they went through a system of narrowing things down to the tribe of the new king, to the family of that tribe of the new king, to the man of the family of the tribe of the new king.

And the name God presented them with was Saul.

But when they called his name, he was not there! In a hilarious twist, look at what happened next:

1 Samuel 10:22 *Therefore they enquired of the LORD further, if the man should yet come thither. And the LORD answered, Behold, he hath hid himself among the stuff.* **23** *And they ran and fetched him thence...*

Their new king, the man they demanded to lead them, was scared and hiding! That should have let them know what they were in for. Later on when Goliath came to battle, Saul "made himself scarce" yet again, and someone else had to fight that battle.

DO realize that external size is no indicator of internal character. Saul was a big man on the outside and a tiny, scared little man on the inside. If all we ever look at is externals, we will miss the greatness of many who seem small and the smallness of many who seem great!

Personal Notes:

_____

_____

_____

_____

_____

_____

_____

_____

_____

_____

_____

_____

_____

_____

_____

_____

_____

_____

_____

_____

_____

_____

_____

_____

_____

_____

_____

_____

Devotion 75

Saul, hide-and-seek Saul, had been found and presented to the people as king. The monarchy of Israel had begun; the question was, now what?

1 Samuel 10:25 *Then Samuel told the people the manner of the kingdom, and wrote it in a book, and laid it up before the LORD. And Samuel sent all the people away, every man to his house.* **26** *And Saul also went home to Gibeah; and there went with him a band of men, whose hearts God had touched.* **27** *But the children of Belial said, How shall this man save us? And they despised him, and brought him no presents. But he held his peace.*

Though God had not wanted them to have a king quite yet, He gave them one nonetheless. But then He in mercy went even a step further and reached out to touch the hearts of the men of Israel to follow the new king. When that happened, two different responses, two different kinds of men, emerged.

There were those whose hearts the Lord touched, and there were those who would not respond. They were called "Children of Belial," meaning vain, profane people. They "despised" Saul and disrespected the new king both by speaking against him and also by not bringing him a present to help his kingdom rule get up and running.

How did Saul respond to that insulting treatment? He held his peace.

How different from Saul in the established years of his monarchy, when even perceived insults that were not really real drew his full wrath and ire!

DO be in the habit of letting some things go. If you spend your life responding to every insult and slight, you will never accomplish much. No freight train would ever get to its destination if it stopped to argue with every Chihuahua barking at it as it rolls down the tracks!

Personal Notes:

_____

_____

_____

_____

_____

_____

_____

_____

_____

_____

_____

_____

_____

_____

_____

_____

_____

_____

_____

_____

_____

_____

_____

_____

_____

Devotion 76

After Saul was anointed king, everyone went back to their lives and businesses. But though the people of Israel did not seem to understand the significance of the change that had just taken place, the nations around them certainly did. Israel was "just like them" now. They used to be ruled by God; now, they had a human king. And that made them, in the eyes of some, ripe for the picking.

1 Samuel 11:1 *Then Nahash the Ammonite came up, and encamped against Jabeshgilead: and all the men of Jabesh said unto Nahash, Make a covenant with us, and we will serve thee.*

When the Ammonites came to besiege Jabesh, the people in the city quickly asked for terms of peace. Fighting did not even occur to them. But the terms of peace were unbelievably harsh.

1 Samuel 11:2 *And Nahash the Ammonite answered them, On this condition will I make a covenant with you, that I may thrust out all your right eyes, and lay it for a reproach upon all Israel.*

Harsh? Yes. Cruel? Yes again. Pointless? No, definitely not.

Warriors in those days held their shield in the left hand and looked out past it with the right eye. To take a person's right eye rendered them forever incapable of fighting. Nahash did not mind these people living; he just wanted to make sure they could never fight again.

The devil does not mind you living; he just doesn't want you fighting him. Just go along with wickedness, and he will leave you alone! But God called us to be soldiers of Christ (2 Timothy 2:3), so for a child of God, that is simply not an option.

DO make the devil miserable; fight, stand for righteousness, make your voice heard!

Personal Notes:

_____

_____

_____

_____

_____

_____

_____

_____

_____

_____

_____

_____

_____

_____

_____

_____

_____

_____

_____

_____

_____

_____

_____

_____

Devotion 77

When Nahash laid his terrible terms of peace on the residents of Jabesh, they told him that if no one came to save them in seven days, they would agree. So they sent messengers throughout all Israel to see if anyone would come to save them. It is ironic that they did not even seem to think of sending messengers to the new king; it seems that not many people were impressed with the "big guy."

Nonetheless, word did get to him. And when it did, he blew a gasket, and it is a good thing that he did:

1 Samuel 11:6 *And the Spirit of God came upon Saul when he heard those tidings, and his anger was kindled greatly. 7 And he took a yoke of oxen, and hewed them in pieces, and sent them throughout all the coasts of Israel by the hands of messengers, saying, Whosoever cometh not forth after Saul and after Samuel, so shall it be done unto his oxen. And the fear of the LORD fell on the people, and they came out with one consent.*

Saul got angry, really, really angry. And it was his anger that moved the people to come out and fight for their brethren! Saul could have asked nicely all day, he could have patiently explained the need, and all he would have gotten were polite responses that people already had plans, they had to rewind their 8-track tapes that day, there was laundry to do.

There are times when anger is actually the appropriate response. Jesus got angry enough to flip tables and chase people with whips. Paul threatened to come to the church at Corinth with a rod in his hand. Aged John threatened Diotrephes.

DO have your temper under control, but DO also understand that there are times to get angry! Only a coward refuses to get angry under any circumstances, and God never called us to be cowards.

Personal Notes:

_____

_____

_____

_____

_____

_____

_____

_____

_____

_____

_____

_____

_____

_____

_____

_____

_____

_____

_____

_____

_____

_____

_____

_____

Devotion 78

When Saul, in his great anger sent his message for Israel to come out after him to fight for Jabesh, 330,000 men responded to the call. One day after that, they were descending on the Ammonites gathered around Jabesh besieging it, and the battle was on.

1 Samuel 11:11 *And it was so on the morrow, that Saul put the people in three companies; and they came into the midst of the host in the morning watch, and slew the Ammonites until the heat of the day: and it came to pass, that they which remained were scattered, so that two of them were not left together.*

This was a great victory and a tremendous start to the monarchy. But there was still no real sense of unity in the land:

1 Samuel 11:12 *And the people said unto Samuel, Who is he that said, Shall Saul reign over us? bring the men, that we may put them to death.*

They have just saved many of their countrymen from death or a fate about as bad as death, and their idea of a celebration is...wait for it...to call for the death of some of their countrymen. Fortunately, Saul was having none of that:

1 Samuel 11:13 *And Saul said, There shall not a man be put to death this day: for to day the LORD hath wrought salvation in Israel.*

Good for you, Saul.

DO realize that vengeance is never the goal; coming together to do a work for God is the goal! Saul could have held a grudge over past insults, but instead, he chose to move past that and glorify the Lord.

Personal Notes:

_____
_____
_____
_____
_____
_____
_____
_____
_____
_____
_____
_____
_____
_____
_____
_____
_____
_____
_____
_____
_____
_____
_____
_____
_____
_____
_____

Devotion 79

The king was now acknowledged by all the nation, and it was time for Samuel to begin saying his goodbyes. Look at what he said as he addressed the people he had led practically since his childhood.

1 Samuel 12:1 *And Samuel said unto all Israel, Behold, I have hearkened unto your voice in all that ye said unto me, and have made a king over you. 2 And now, behold, the king walketh before you: and I am old and grayheaded; and, behold, my sons are with you: and I have walked before you from my childhood unto this day. 3 Behold, here I am: witness against me before the LORD, and before his anointed: whose ox have I taken? or whose ass have I taken? or whom have I defrauded? whom have I oppressed? or of whose hand have I received any bribe to blind mine eyes therewith? and I will restore it you. 4 And they said, Thou hast not defrauded us, nor oppressed us, neither hast thou taken ought of any man's hand.*

Out of an entire lifetime, not one person was able to rightly accuse Samuel of any wrongdoing. What a testimony!

Everyone will have people who do not like them. Many will even have people lie about them. But the goal of every one of us ought to be to live our lives in such an honorable way that, if people are honest, they have to admit that we have done right all the way through.

DO be that honorable; the two kinds of people that will always be remembered are the very dishonorable and the very honorable, but only the very honorable will be remembered with fondness!

Personal Notes:

_____

_____

_____

_____

_____

_____

_____

_____

_____

_____

_____

_____

_____

_____

_____

_____

_____

_____

_____

_____

_____

_____

_____

_____

_____

_____

_____

Devotion 80

After Samuel called the entire nation to give witness to whether or not he had consistently done right among them, and after they clearly gave testimony to how honorable he had been, he gave them a short history lesson. This history lesson in 1 Samuel 12:6-12 consisted of how disobedient they had been as a people for generation after generation. He capped the lesson with how wrong they had been to ask for a king.

That damage was done, but how to go on forward was the question. Here is the answer that Samuel gave them:

1 Samuel 12:14 *If ye will fear the LORD, and serve him, and obey his voice, and not rebel against the commandment of the LORD, then shall both ye and also the king that reigneth over you continue following the LORD your God:* **15** *But if ye will not obey the voice of the LORD, but rebel against the commandment of the LORD, then shall the hand of the LORD be against you, as it was against your fathers.*

The way to go forward was to go forward. Samuel told them to "continue following the LORD your God." They could not undo a single thing they had done. But they could go on and do right from there.

When you do wrong, the bell usually cannot be unrung. But what can always be done is to do right every day thereafter. No matter what you have done wrong previously in your life, the right response is for you to get right with God, and DO right every single day thereafter.

Personal Notes:

Devotion 81

Samuel was intent on giving the people one more reminder of how wrong they had been to ask for a king, and this time it would be a startling visual reminder:

1 Samuel 12:16 *Now therefore stand and see this great thing, which the LORD will do before your eyes. **17** Is it not wheat harvest to day? I will call unto the LORD, and he shall send thunder and rain; that ye may perceive and see that your wickedness is great, which ye have done in the sight of the LORD, in asking you a king. **18** So Samuel called unto the LORD; and the LORD sent thunder and rain that day: and all the people greatly feared the LORD and Samuel. **19** And all the people said unto Samuel, Pray for thy servants unto the LORD thy God, that we die not: for we have added unto all our sins this evil, to ask us a king.*

Rain was almost entirely unknown during the time of the wheat harvest; it simply did not happen much. And such a violent rain as Samuel called for was clearly a miraculous sign from the Lord of His displeasure with the people. Seeing this, the people asked Samuel to pray for them. Look at his response:

1 Samuel 12:23 *Moreover as for me, God forbid that I should sin against the LORD in ceasing to pray for you: but I will teach you the good and the right way:*

Samuel regarded it as a sin for him to stop praying for the people! No matter what they had done, he would continue to pray for them. Only in the book of Jeremiah do we ever find God commanding His man not to pray for the people.

DO understand that there will rarely ever be a time when it is right to stop praying for people! It may be right to stop associating with them or to stop helping them in some way, but DO continue to pray!

Personal Notes:

_____

_____

_____

_____

_____

_____

_____

_____

_____

_____

_____

_____

_____

_____

_____

_____

_____

_____

_____

_____

_____

_____

_____

_____

_____

Devotion 82

King Saul reigned for two relatively quiet, obedient years. But then his spiral into self-will and disobedience began. The Philistines came to battle against Israel, and Samuel told Saul to wait until a certain day and that he would come and offer sacrifice before Israel joined the battle. But something delayed Samuel by just a few minutes:

1 Samuel 13:8 *And he tarried seven days, according to the set time that Samuel had appointed: but Samuel came not to Gilgal; and the people were scattered from him.*

Seeing the people beginning to scatter, Saul determined to take matters into his own hands.

1 Samuel 13:9 *And Saul said, Bring hither a burnt offering to me, and peace offerings. And he offered the burnt offering.*

This was not his place. He was the King, not a priest. And because of this disobedience, taking the role of the priesthood unto himself, Samuel gave a word from the Lord to him, a word that he did not want to hear:

1 Samuel 13:13 *And Samuel said to Saul, Thou hast done foolishly: thou hast not kept the commandment of the LORD thy God, which he commanded thee: for now would the LORD have established thy kingdom upon Israel for ever. 14 But now thy kingdom shall not continue: the LORD hath sought him a man after his own heart, and the LORD hath commanded him to be captain over his people, because thou hast not kept that which the LORD commanded thee.*

God was not looking for a man who would "take everything up on his own shoulders;" he was looking for a man "after his own heart."

DO realize that while we as God's children have a great many responsibilities, the greatest responsibility we have is to make sure that our heart lines up with His heart on everything!

Personal Notes:

_____

_____

_____

_____

_____

_____

_____

_____

_____

_____

_____

_____

_____

_____

_____

_____

_____

_____

_____

_____

_____

_____

Devotion 83

As the battle continued long against the Philistines, the text of Scripture gives us a commentary as to the state of battle readiness of the children of Israel, and it is not a good commentary.

1 Samuel 13:19 *Now there was no smith found throughout all the land of Israel: for the Philistines said, Lest the Hebrews make them swords or spears:* **20** *But all the Israelites went down to the Philistines, to sharpen every man his share, and his coulter, and his axe, and his mattock.* **21** *Yet they had a file for the mattocks, and for the coulters, and for the forks, and for the axes, and to sharpen the goads.* **22** *So it came to pass in the day of battle, that there was neither sword nor spear found in the hand of any of the people that were with Saul and Jonathan: but with Saul and with Jonathan his son was there found.*

Simply put, the Philistines had disarmed the Israelites. In the entire country, the only people with sword and spear were King Saul and his son Jonathan.

Both physically and spiritually, there is a great lesson to learn there. There are words for people who have been disarmed: victims and slaves.

In our country today, there is a cry for disarmament both physically and spiritually. Spiritually the forces of wickedness desire to take away from us an absolute confidence in Scripture, a walk with God, and a strong local church. Physically, the forces of wickedness desire to take firearms out of the hands of law-abiding citizens. DO realize that in either case, the end result will be victimhood and slavery!

Personal Notes:

_____
_____
_____
_____
_____
_____
_____
_____
_____
_____
_____
_____
_____
_____
_____
_____
_____
_____
_____
_____
_____
_____
_____
_____
_____

Devotion 84

Though Saul was the king of Israel, the long war with the Philistines began to show that he was not the best man in his house. His son Jonathan, the man who because of his father's sin would never be king, quickly began to distinguish himself as a man of great worth.

1 Samuel 14:6 *And Jonathan said to the young man that bare his armour, Come, and let us go over unto the garrison of these uncircumcised: it may be that the LORD will work for us: for there is no restraint to the LORD to save by many or by few.* **7** *And his armourbearer said unto him, Do all that is in thine heart: turn thee; behold, I am with thee according to thy heart.*

In these two verses, we find a wealth of information about Jonathan. We find that Jonathan had a fierce trust in the Lord. With only one man by his side and one weapon, he determined to go attack a Philistine garrison simply because he had confidence in the Lord God.

We also find that Jonathan was a decent theologian. He said, "There is no restraint to the LORD to save by many or by few." Jonathan was giving testimony to the omnipotence of God.

We then find that Jonathan was a good leader of men. His armourbearer said, "Do all that is in thine heart: turn thee; behold, I am with thee according to thy heart."

All of that, and yet Jonathan would never be king. The disobedience of his father marred the future of the son.

Do you want your children to have the best possible future? Then DO make sure that <u>you</u> do everything right. If there is anyone our disobedience will affect, those in our family will inevitably be first on the list!

Personal Notes:

_____
_____
_____
_____
_____
_____
_____
_____
_____
_____
_____
_____
_____
_____
_____
_____
_____
_____
_____
_____
_____
_____
_____
_____

Devotion 85

When Jonathan and his armor bearer determined to attack the Philistines, things quickly went their way:

1 Samuel 14:13 *And Jonathan climbed up upon his hands and upon his feet, and his armourbearer after him: and they fell before Jonathan; and his armourbearer slew after him.* **14** *And that first slaughter, which Jonathan and his armourbearer made, was about twenty men, within as it were an half acre of land, which a yoke of oxen might plow.*

Two men killed twenty. That in and of itself was a great victory, but the aftershock was much larger.

1 Samuel 14:15 *And there was trembling in the host, in the field, and among all the people: the garrison, and the spoilers, they also trembled, and the earth quaked: so it was a very great trembling.* **16** *And the watchmen of Saul in Gibeah of Benjamin looked; and, behold, the multitude melted away, and they went on beating down one another.*

Between the shaking of the frightened Philistines and an earthquake whose timing clearly marks it as supernatural, the Philistines went into such a panic that they lost all composure, and actually turned their swords on one another.

In other words, there is a good lesson here that we can learn from bad people: panic is always an enemy, never an ally.

Disasters do not usually announce themselves well ahead of time. Therefore, we must mentally and emotionally prepare for them in anticipation of the fact that they will come, and usually at the worst possible time. DO determine that you will keep your wits when all around you are losing theirs; there is nothing that is ever made better by panicking!

Personal Notes:

_____

_____

_____

_____

_____

_____

_____

_____

_____

_____

_____

_____

_____

_____

_____

_____

_____

_____

_____

_____

_____

_____

_____

_____

_____

_____

Devotion 86

As the Philistines panicked at their initial defeat at the hands of Jonathan and his armor bearer, the noise of the tumult reached the ears of Saul. He quickly took steps to find out what was going on and who was responsible; in verse eighteen, he told Ahiah, the priest, to bring the Ark.

Saul wanted Ahiah the priest to do something very spiritual; he wanted him to inquire of God and find out what he should do. But what happens next is very instructive:

1 Samuel 14:19 *And it came to pass, while Saul talked unto the priest, that the noise that was in the host of the Philistines went on and increased: and Saul said unto the priest, Withdraw thine hand.* **20** *And Saul and all the people that were with him assembled themselves, and they came to the battle: and, behold, every man's sword was against his fellow, and there was a very great discomfiture.*

In the middle of "praying," it became clear that there was a battle for life and death going on. So Saul told the priest to stop what he was doing, and all of the men of war rushed out to battle.

How interesting to realize that there is a time to be still and pray, and there is also a time to set prayer aside in favor of battle!

Some years ago, a rather poor excuse for a husband told me that if someone broke into his home to assault his wife and children, he would pray. I told him that I would pray too; "Lord, please don't let me miss with a single shot!"

DO understand that pacifism is not biblical. Especially when it comes to innocent wives and children, the good God of heaven gave those wives and children husbands and fathers so that there would be someone there to do violence on their behalf should they ever be threatened. I would hate to stand before God one day and have Him say, "Why did you allow the precious child I gave you to be hurt?" and then try to explain to Him that, "I prayed while it was happening."

Personal Notes:

_____

_____

_____

_____

_____

_____

_____

_____

_____

_____

_____

_____

_____

_____

_____

_____

_____

_____

_____

_____

_____

_____

_____

Devotion 87

Thanks to the initiative of Jonathan, the children of Israel ended up winning an utterly improbable victory against the Philistines. But it is what the text of Scripture says immediately following that is very instructive:

1 Samuel 14:21 *Moreover the Hebrews that were with the Philistines before that time, which went up with them into the camp from the country round about, even they also turned to be with the Israelites that were with Saul and Jonathan.*

Samuel here drew a distinction between Hebrews and Israelites, one of only two places in Scripture where that clear distinction is made, 2 Corinthians 11:22 being the other. We normally think of those two things as being synonymous. But in this particular case, a very stark distinction was drawn.

There were people descended from Abraham (Hebrews) that nonetheless were not given the honor of being regarded as Israelites. Israelites referred to the nation God had built and to those who gave that nation their loyalty. These Hebrews had, at some point, gone over to the Philistines, and only now when the Philistines began to lose did they turn and side with their own countrymen.

It is good that they did, but it is also an example of expedience rather than loyalty. Those who were loyal were true to Israel even when it looked like they would always be on the losing side.

Very few things in life are as precious as loyalty! DO be loyal to God and your church and your family; never allow future generations to speak or write of you as a fair-weather friend.

Personal Notes:

_____
_____
_____
_____
_____
_____
_____
_____
_____
_____
_____
_____
_____
_____
_____
_____
_____
_____
_____
_____
_____
_____
_____
_____
_____
_____
_____
_____

Devotion 88

When the Israelites started winning, people who had been in hiding came out of the woodwork to join the battle. It seemed that nothing could go wrong, and then Saul opened his mouth.

1 Samuel 14:24 *And the men of Israel were distressed that day: for Saul had adjured the people, saying, Cursed be the man that eateth any food until evening, that I may be avenged on mine enemies. So none of the people tasted any food.*

Please allow me to give you the entire list of why this was a good idea:

There it is.

This was a horrible idea with a horrible motive. Saul, in his words, wanted vengeance on his enemies and was willing to make his own people hungry and weak to get what he wanted. If he had been thinking about those he was leading rather than thinking about himself, he never would have done something so foolish.

DO put others first, especially those that you are leading. If you keep them strong, they will keep you strong!

Personal Notes:

Devotion 89

The battle against the Philistines was still raging on, and the people were growing weaker and weaker because of Saul's foolish command. But Jonathan, who knew nothing of what his father had said, ended up violating that foolish command.

1 Samuel 14:26 *And when the people were come into the wood, behold, the honey dropped; but no man put his hand to his mouth: for the people feared the oath.* **27** *But Jonathan heard not when his father charged the people with the oath: wherefore he put forth the end of the rod that was in his hand, and dipped it in an honeycomb, and put his hand to his mouth; and his eyes were enlightened.*

When people are weak, we Christians often make the mistake of spiritualizing everything. And while many issues certainly are spiritual, sometimes things boil down to physical issues. Jonathan had something to eat, and it strengthened him. When the text tells us that "his eyes were enlightened," we would say, "his face lit up."

Being a Christian in a non-Christian world is hard enough. It is even harder when we combine poor habits physically with the spiritual battles we face day by day.

DO pray and read your Bible and everything else that is of a spiritual nature for a child of God. But DO also eat right and exercise and get enough rest. Never make the spiritual harder by being foolish in the physical!

Personal Notes:

Devotion 90

After Jonathan unknowingly disobeyed his father's foolish command, the people quickly spoke up to tell him what he had done.

1 Samuel 14:28 *Then answered one of the people, and said, Thy father straitly charged the people with an oath, saying, Cursed be the man that eateth any food this day. And the people were faint.*

They told him what his father said, but they were weak to the point of exhaustion because of it, and Jonathan could see that.

1 Samuel 14:29 *Then said Jonathan, My father hath troubled the land: see, I pray you, how mine eyes have been enlightened, because I tasted a little of this honey.* **30** *How much more, if haply the people had eaten freely to day of the spoil of their enemies which they found? for had there not been now a much greater slaughter among the Philistines?*

There was no disrespect in anything that Jonathan said, merely an accurate assessment of how foolish his father's command was and the damage that it caused. And I find it very refreshing that he was willing to acknowledge the fault in someone closest to him rather than playing the part of a blind loyalist. Anyone can find fault in "others;" it takes a good bit of character to recognize the faults of yourself and those closest to you.

DO have that good bit of character!

Personal Notes:

_____
_____
_____
_____
_____
_____
_____
_____
_____
_____
_____
_____
_____
_____
_____
_____
_____
_____
_____
_____
_____
_____
_____
_____
_____
_____
_____

Devotion 91

After Jonathan rightly noted how his father's foolish command had weakened the people, the people continued to fight the battle on an empty stomach. But finally they got so weak and famished that they did the unthinkable:

1 Samuel 14:32 *And the people flew upon the spoil, and took sheep, and oxen, and calves, and slew them on the ground: and the people did eat them with the blood.*

This was one of the greatest sins under the Mosaic law:

Leviticus 17:10 *And whatsoever man there be of the house of Israel, or of the strangers that sojourn among you, that eateth any manner of blood; I will even set my face against that soul that eateth blood, and will cut him off from among his people.* **11** *For the life of the flesh is in the blood: and I have given it to you upon the altar to make an atonement for your souls: for it is the blood that maketh an atonement for the soul.*

When Saul realized this, he told the people that they had sinned, then he cooked the meat for them. Huge sin, very laid-back response. But shortly after that, he found out that Jonathan had eaten a little bit of honey, and his answer to him in verse forty-four was "thou shalt surely die, Jonathan."

The people had "merely" disobeyed the Lord; Jonathan had embarrassed his father. Do you see the skewed priorities of Saul? And yet how often do we yawn when people sin against God and fly into a rage when they hurt our precious feelings?

DO recognize the difference between sins against God and personal embarrassment against us. Had it not been for the intervention of the people, Saul would have lost his own son due to his misplaced priorities!

Personal Notes:

_____

_____

_____

_____

_____

_____

_____

_____

_____

_____

_____

_____

_____

_____

_____

_____

_____

_____

_____

_____

_____

_____

_____

Devotion 92

1 Samuel 15:1 *Samuel also said unto Saul, The LORD sent me to anoint thee to be king over his people, over Israel: now therefore hearken thou unto the voice of the words of the LORD.* **2** *Thus saith the LORD of hosts, I remember that which Amalek did to Israel, how he laid wait for him in the way, when he came up from Egypt.* **3** *Now go and smite Amalek, and utterly destroy all that they have, and spare them not; but slay both man and woman, infant and suckling, ox and sheep, camel and ass.*

When we come to verses like these, our heart instinctively breaks to see the command that everyone be slain, right down to the children. And yet, as always, there is a righteous reason for everything God does.

Samuel hearkened back to what Amalek did to Israel when they came up out of Egypt. Here is a bit more detail on that:

Deuteronomy 25:17 *Remember what Amalek did unto thee by the way, when ye were come forth out of Egypt;* **18** *How he met thee by the way, and smote the hindmost of thee, even all that were feeble behind thee, when thou wast faint and weary; and he feared not God.*

When Israel was at their lowest point, Amalek snuck up behind them and murdered the weakest of them. God would not forget that, and now was the time for judgment to fall because of it.

But it was not just a matter of what happened in the past that precipitated this command. The book of Esther, written hundreds of years later, shows a descendant of Amalek trying to kill every Jew on the face of the earth, thousands of years before Hitler ever conceived of such horror. This command that God gave, had it been fully obeyed, would have stopped that near Holocaust from ever even beginning.

DO realize that everything God does or commands has a reason, even if we, in our day, will never understand it. He has never been anything but good to us, so trust even when you cannot comprehend!

Personal Notes:

_____
_____
_____
_____
_____
_____
_____
_____
_____
_____
_____
_____
_____
_____
_____
_____
_____
_____
_____
_____
_____

Devotion 93

Having been clearly commanded to destroy Amalek and everything they possessed, Saul had no excuse for anything but full obedience. But, after winning the battle, Saul decided that he had a "better idea" than God:

1 Samuel 15:8 *And he took Agag the king of the Amalekites alive, and utterly destroyed all the people with the edge of the sword.* **9** *But Saul and the people spared Agag, and the best of the sheep, and of the oxen, and of the fatlings, and the lambs, and all that was good, and would not utterly destroy them: but every thing that was vile and refuse, that they destroyed utterly.*

When Samuel showed up, Saul quickly found out that God was not impressed with his "better idea."

1 Samuel 15:18 *And the LORD sent thee on a journey, and said, Go and utterly destroy the sinners the Amalekites, and fight against them until they be consumed.* **19** *Wherefore then didst thou not obey the voice of the LORD, but didst fly upon the spoil, and didst evil in the sight of the LORD?*

Repeat after me: "I do not have a better idea than God; I do not have a better idea than God; I do not have a better idea than God."

DO remember that you will never have a better idea than God!

Personal Notes:

_____
_____
_____
_____
_____
_____
_____
_____
_____
_____
_____
_____
_____
_____
_____
_____
_____
_____
_____
_____
_____
_____
_____
_____
_____
_____
_____
_____

Devotion 94

As Samuel continued to confront Saul over his disobedience, Saul did what so many people are prone to do; he began to make excuses and even to couch them in religious reasoning:

1 Samuel 15:20 *And Saul said unto Samuel, Yea, I have obeyed the voice of the LORD, and have gone the way which the LORD sent me, and have brought Agag the king of Amalek, and have utterly destroyed the Amalekites.* **21** *But the people took of the spoil, sheep and oxen, the chief of the things which should have been utterly destroyed, to sacrifice unto the LORD thy God in Gilgal.*

"I kept that stuff so I could put it in the offering plate, Samuel! That makes it okay, right?"

No. No, it doesn't.

1 Samuel 15:22 *And Samuel said, Hath the LORD as great delight in burnt offerings and sacrifices, as in obeying the voice of the LORD? Behold, to obey is better than sacrifice, and to hearken than the fat of rams.* **23** *For rebellion is as the sin of witchcraft, and stubbornness is as iniquity and idolatry. Because thou hast rejected the word of the LORD, he hath also rejected thee from being king.*

Witchcraft was one of only a very small handful of things in the Old Testament that brought the death penalty. But rebellion is so abhorrent in the sight of God that He placed it in the same category as witchcraft!

There is nothing more disgusting to God than a stubborn, unbowed heart and will.

DO make up your mind to bow the knee rather than stiffen the neck to God!

Personal Notes:

_____
_____
_____
_____
_____
_____
_____
_____
_____
_____
_____
_____
_____
_____
_____
_____
_____
_____
_____
_____
_____
_____
_____
_____
_____
_____
_____

Devotion 95

While dealing with Saul about his rebellion, Samuel told him in verse twenty-two that he had "rejected" the word of the Lord, and therefore the Lord had rejected him. Saul, seeing all that he was about to lose, quickly "apologized:"

1 Samuel 15:24 *And Saul said unto Samuel, I have sinned: for I have transgressed the commandment of the LORD, and thy words: because I feared the people, and obeyed their voice.* **25** *Now therefore, I pray thee, pardon my sin, and turn again with me, that I may worship the LORD.*

Notice that in response to Samuel's proclamation that he had rejected the word of the Lord, Saul countered by saying that he had "transgressed" the commandment of the Lord. Those are two very different words with very different meanings. To reject means to loathe something and push it away; to transgress means to step over something, perhaps intentionally, perhaps only accidentally.

Notice how Samuel responded:

1 Samuel 15:26 *And Samuel said unto Saul, I will not return with thee: for thou hast rejected the word of the LORD, and the LORD hath rejected thee from being king over Israel.*

Samuel would not let Saul get by with softening his rejection of God's Word into a mere transgression of God's Word. What Saul did was intentional and was born out of a heart of rebellion, and therefore he could not be helped.

DO examine your heart on a daily basis to make sure there is no attitude of rejection of God's

Word within you. A person merely transgressing can very likely be helped; a person with a rebellious heart, rejecting the Word of God, cannot.

Personal Notes:

_____

_____

_____

_____

_____

_____

_____

_____

_____

_____

_____

_____

_____

_____

_____

_____

_____

_____

_____

_____

_____

_____

_____

_____

_____

_____

_____

Devotion 96

Having given the verdict of his rejection by God, Samuel turned to walk away from Saul. It is then that a bewildering scene took place.

1 Samuel 15:27 *And as Samuel turned about to go away, he laid hold upon the skirt of his mantle, and it rent.* **28** *And Samuel said unto him, The LORD hath rent the kingdom of Israel from thee this day, and hath given it to a neighbour of thine, that is better than thou.* **29** *And also the Strength of Israel will not lie nor repent: for he is not a man, that he should repent.* **30** *Then he said, I have sinned: yet honour me now, I pray thee, before the elders of my people, and before Israel, and turn again with me, that I may worship the LORD thy God.* **31** *So Samuel turned again after Saul; and Saul worshipped the LORD.*

Saul grabbed for Samuel and ended up tearing part of his clothing. Samuel used that as a visual illustration to tell Saul that the Lord had torn the kingdom away from him and give it someone else and would not change his mind.

But it is what Saul did next that is so interesting. Knowing he has lost the kingdom, he still asked Samuel to "honor him" in front of the people and "worship the Lord" with him. Saul was incredibly concerned that no one think badly of him.

When our focus is on making sure that people think well of us rather than having God think well of us, we will be more concerned about hiding our sin and its consequences than we will about not sinning to begin with.

DO check each day what is most important to you, doing right or being perceived as doing right. If you are more concerned about what others think of you than what God thinks of you, some things desperately need to change!

Personal Notes:

_____

_____

_____

_____

_____

_____

_____

_____

_____

_____

_____

_____

_____

_____

_____

_____

_____

_____

_____

_____

_____

_____

_____

_____

_____

_____

_____

_____

_____

Devotion 97

Of all the things that we have the capability to waste, perhaps the worst example of waste is wasted potential. Saul had been rejected by God from the kingship. Samuel had delivered the message. But the last verse of the chapter shows the broken-heartedness associated with all that took place.

1 Samuel 15:35 *And Samuel came no more to see Saul until the day of his death: nevertheless Samuel mourned for Saul: and the LORD repented that he had made Saul king over Israel.*

Samuel was brokenhearted over Saul. The Lord was disgusted with and disappointed by Saul. Saul stood head and shoulders taller than everyone else in Israel; he may well have been the biggest man physically in all of their history. He was a powerful leader. His potential was off the charts. And yet he wasted every bit of that potential with his rebellion and self-will.

God builds into every one of us the potential to do great things for Him. Wasting money is a bad idea, wasting time is a tragedy, but wasting potential is a disaster of epic proportions. Never, ever, allow sin and rebellion in your heart to rob you of the potential that you could fulfill for God. DO live right and up to the maximum potential God has built within you!

Personal Notes:

_____
_____
_____
_____
_____
_____
_____
_____
_____
_____
_____
_____
_____
_____
_____
_____
_____
_____
_____
_____
_____
_____
_____
_____
_____
_____
_____
_____

Other Books by Dr. Bo Wagner

Beyond the Colored Coat
Daniel: Breathtaking
Don't Muzzle the Ox
Esther: Five Feast and the Finger Prints of God
From Footers to Finish Nails
I'm Saved! Now What???
James: The Pen and the Plumb Line
Jonah: A Study in Greatness
Marriage Makers/Marriage Breakers
Nehemiah: A Labor of Love
Romans: Salvation From A-Z
Ruth: Diamonds in the Darkness
DO Drops Volume 1

Fiction Titles

Cry From the Coal Mine (Vol. 1)
Free Fall (Vol. 2)
Broken Brotherhood (Vol. 3)
The Blade of Black Crow (Vol. 4)
Ghost Ship (Vol. 5)
When Serpents Rise (Vol. 6)
Moth Man (Vol. 7)
Runaway (Vol. 8)

Sci-Fi

Zak Blue and the Great Space Chase:
Falcon Wing (Vol. 1)